Contents

Editorial

Fenella Porter and Caroline Sweetman

Gender mainstreaming has been defined as 'a strategy which aims to bring about gender equality and advance women's rights by infusing gender analysis, gender-sensitive research, women's perspectives and gender equality goals into mainstream policies, projects and institutions' (Association for Women's Rights in Development 2004, 1).

Caroline Moser and Annalise Moser (in this issue) suggest that many development organisations have followed the definition set out by the UN Economic and Social Council:

Mainstreaming a gender perspective is the process of assessing the implications for women and men of any planned action, including legislation, policies or programmes, in all areas and at all levels. It is a strategy for making women's as well as men's concerns and experiences an integral dimension of the design, implementation, monitoring and evaluation of policies and programmes in all political, economic and societal spheres so that women and men benefit equally and inequality is not perpetuated. The ultimate goal is to achieve gender equality (1997, 28).

Contributors to this collection of articles were briefed to look very critically at how gender mainstreaming has been carried out in organisations involved in the development process, to assess the difference that gender mainstreaming has made, and to suggest ways of overcoming the challenges.

Different contributions focus on international, national or local levels, and within government and NGOs. We believe that a decade after gender mainstreaming entered the development lexicon,[1] this reflection and analysis is critical. What are the barriers against and facilitating factors in favour of ensuring development in the interests of women? Does gender mainstreaming in development organisations deserve its poor image among many in the international women's movement?

Integrationist and agenda-setting approaches to mainstreaming

Rounaq Jahan, a researcher into gender mainstreaming, found it helpful to distinguish between two kinds of mainstreaming: integrationist and agenda-setting (Jahan 1995, 13).

Jahan suggests that integationist approaches, which began during the UN Decade for Women 1976–85, aim to integrate women, as well as men, into the existing development framework. Integration leads to a focus on women as a marginalised group; as people with additional or special interests. Male interests remain viewed as the norm. This approach has been criticised by feminists as amounting to a recipe in which an extra ingredient is added: 'add women and stir'. Yet the end result of the recipe, and the cooking method, remain basically the same. This form of gender mainstreaming can be seen in the welfare, anti-poverty, and efficiency approaches to women in development (WID), which were identified by Moser (1989). Women are the focus of concern because they are perceived as an especially needy target group, and/or because of the contribution they can make to development that is directed by development organisations which are intrinsically 'male-biased' (Elson 1991). This sort of approach is politically conservative, ignoring unequal gender power relations, often misunderstanding the existing economic role of women in so-called developing countries.

The interests that women share as members of a sub-dominant social group have been labelled 'strategic gender interests' by Molyneux (1985), indicating interests through which women can achieve change in their overall position in society. Such interests have been furthered through equity approaches to women in development (Moser 1989), which aim to transform law, customs, and institutional procedures so that these no longer discriminate against women on grounds of sex. Women's interests may also be served by empowerment approaches, which aim to support women at community level to further their own strategic gender interests, as well as to further their more immediate practical interests by obtaining sufficient resources to enable them to put their ideas and choices into action (Kabeer 1999).

Yet it seems that development interventions which genuinely support the empowerment of women – as individuals who should be in charge of their own destinies, and as a collective marginalised social group – are rare. Rather than gender mainstreaming leading to transformed development, 'gender' has itself been transformed — as a field of research and action, it has been depoliticised (Pearson 1999). The agenda of the international women's movement as regards development was summed up in the UN International Women's Year (1975) as equality, development, and peace. The ideal of economic development which does not occur at the expense of equality and peace is still unrealised. Many argue that such ideals have been distorted in the process of integration of gender issues into the pre-existing mandates, ideologies, and procedures of development organisations (Kardam 1993; Miller 1998).

What is the answer? Should we forget gender mainstreaming, or should we continue the struggle to achieve what Jahan describes as a more radical, agenda-setting kind of gender mainstreaming? In place of integration, Jahan suggests that transformatory gender mainstreaming is also possible. This aims to 'transform… the existing development agenda' (Jahan 1995). Transformation starts from a gender analysis of inequalities between women and men, which understands gender relations as intersecting with relations of race and class, to create context-specific locations of inequality.

If development organisations carry out gender analysis in this way, new priorities emerge naturally. Development programmes would be informed by an awareness of the political causes of women's marginalisation, and a commitment to support social transformation by challenging gender inequality. For example, the practical problems of poverty faced by female-headed households in rural areas of Africa are shown in gender analysis to be caused, in part, by unequal access to essential resources like land. Thus, on the one hand, gender mainstreaming consists of infusing gender analysis into work being done already in development (for example, land reform). On the other hand it consists of undertaking 'stand alone' work to address particular issues of strategic importance to women, which would not otherwise be undertaken as part of a development agenda (such as addressing violence against women, and sexual and reproductive rights).

Articles in this issue suggest that many organisations which have attempted gender mainstreaming have not moved beyond the integrationist approach. But agenda-setting gender mainstreaming is desperately needed, because women are still as marginalised and excluded as ever from political and economic life. We cannot ignore the central role that governments and NGOs play in this marginalisation and exclusion, and the potential they hold for social, economic, and political transformation in women's lives.

Institutional and operational gender mainstreaming

A second useful distinction made by Jahan (1995) is between institutional and operational gender mainstreaming activities. This is not an 'either/or' option. Gender mainstreaming should involve both kinds of activity, and indeed cannot succeed otherwise. Institutional activities address the internal dynamics of development organisations: their policies, structures, systems, and procedures. Operational activities address the need to change the programmes of work in which the organisation is engaged (ibid.). All articles in this issue focus to some extent on successes and failures of institutionalising gender concerns into development. Caroline and Annalise Moser (this issue) suggest that this side of the equation has taken up most attention to date. In contrast, little is yet known of the impact of gender mainstreaming efforts on the lives of women who are involved with operational development work. They suggest that this needs much more investigation in the years ahead.

Operational mainstreaming: what are the challenges?

The litmus test of successful gender mainstreaming in operational work is that development programmes support the two complementary goals of structural gender equality in society, and the empowerment of women living in poverty. The need to pay

much more attention to the impact of gender mainstreaming on women themselves is amplified by articles from Vandana Desai, and Senorina Wendoh and Tina Wallace, in their articles. But in assessing impact, development workers should adopt a nuanced understanding of the multiple factors which contribute to women's impoverishment and lack of choices. Imported, blueprint analyses and quick-fix solutions suggested by donors with little knowledge of local realities cannot be expected to yield useful analysis. Nor will they be embraced readily by women — or men – working at the local level, who can see that such tools are either wholly inappropriate, or too crude, for the job they have to do.

A key challenge faced in gender mainstreaming in grassroots community development work is inadequate understanding of the tension which exists between supporting the empowerment of women as a sex, and supporting the empowerment of individual women and their households. Approaches to gender and development at this level often fail to deal with the issue of differences between women, whose experience of marginalisation on grounds of sex varies dramatically according to other aspects of identity, including relative wealth or poverty, ethnicity, caste or other factors. These concerns have been critically evaluated by authors including Cornwall (2001). A uni-dimensional analysis of male-to-female oppression does not equip gender and development practitioners to analyse and address the complex relations of power, which constrain the agency of individual women. What is more, sometimes difference can create obstacles to political action to further gender equality. If women do not feel particularly disadvantaged by gender concerns they may – quite legitimately! – pursue other priorities.

As Vandana Desai points out in her article on NGO work in Mumbai, these issues create real challenges for organisations committed to gender mainstreaming. What is needed is operational gender mainstreaming which addresses gender interests as these intersect with other interests, for example caste or age. Operational gender mainstreaming should start with women identifying their own political priorities and strategies.

We believe that development organisations wanting to challenge gender-based discrimination, and improve the lives of individual women in communities, need to adopt a dual-faceted approach. This is to support feminist activity at all levels of society, to ensure that individual women's choices are not constrained by institutional discrimination against them on grounds of their sex. At the same time, support is required for individual women within communities. For many, acute poverty constrains them from embarking on any activity which is not immediately necessary for survival. For this reason, targeting resources on women needs to be seen in context, as part of a commitment to the empowerment of women (Kabeer 1999). In her article in this issue, Elsa Dawson makes this point in the context of an analysis of gender mainstreaming in Oxfam GB. Once immediate survival needs are satisfied, women may opt to pursue political action to ensure that obstacles to future choices are removed. Of course, for some women in some contexts, political action (which may or may not be feminist) may appear to be the fastest route to gain essential resources. But the important point is that it is for women to decide these things for themselves. The role of a development organisation is limited to responding to women's own agendas, in as transformative a way as possible (Young 1993). Development work with women living in poverty should be informed by accurate analysis of the political location of women, and a commitment to supporting the goal of gender equality, as far as is possible.

Without this dual commitment to the empowerment of women and structural gender equality, community-level development work may not even identify the interests that women share on account of their marginalised position in society. Suzanne Clisby's article in this issue highlights the fact that efforts to mainstream gender into local governance in Bolivia failed to create opportunities for women to participate as equals and bring gender issues to the fore. This is because mixed community groups contain power relationships, between women and women, and between women and men, that will privilege the concerns of the most powerful. In such a situation, women's shared gender interests are not likely to be included on the group agenda.

Institutional mainstreaming: assessing the progress

For successful operational gender mainstreaming to take place, changes are required within the institutions of development. Transforming organisations to enable women to participate as fully as men, in terms of numbers and substantive input, is critical for several reasons.

The first of these reasons is the inherent question of justice for women. Women have the right to participate in equal numbers with men throughout society, and this includes within social institutions of government and in NGOs. Another reason is that it is widely believed that women's equal participation affects the agendas of development organisations, making these reflect gender concerns. Care should be taken not to assume that there is a connection between being a woman and furthering the shared strategic interests of women; yet the evidence still shows that it is fair to 'generally assume that feminism is practised by women, and certainly is defined by women's experiences' (Porter 1999, 5). If institutions reform to ensure that women are able to take a full and equal role as decision makers, researchers, planners, and implementers in development, 'women [will] not only become a part of the mainstream, they also reorient the nature of the mainstream' (Jahan 1995, 13).

Yet some critiques of gender mainstreaming point out that ensuring that women participate equally with men is not in itself sufficient to guarantee that organisations address gender inequality in their operations, or internally within their own culture, structure, systems, and procedures. As Aruna Rao and David Kelleher argue in their article, it is not enough to change the identity of the players in the game; it is also necessary to change the rules of the game. Cultural norms from surrounding society are reflected in the practices and values of organisations. To change the practices and values involves the difficult task of challenging formerly unquestioned norms. Rao and Kelleher's iceberg image demonstrates clearly how there are different levels at which change must take place, if organisations are to address gender inequality successfully in their work and in their own internal practices. Only a small proportion of these levels is actually 'visible' above the surface as formal rules. Other levels are 'submerged', and therefore hidden from view. Change at these invisible levels is, nevertheless, essential.

Elsa Dawson's article focuses on Oxfam GB's experience of gender mainstreaming in its South American programme. The emphasis of Oxfam's gender mainstreaming strategy for the region prioritised institutional change. Elsa Dawson challenges the dichotomy between institutional and operational approaches to mainstreaming. For her, gender mainstreaming involves developing contextually appropriate, locally owned understandings of gender relations at every level of programme planning and implementation. She maintains that this should be the responsibility of everyone involved in planning and carrying out development work. Carrying out a gender analysis as a separate specialist task can undermine the degree of ownership felt by staff in the organisation.

The role of agents in mainstreaming

Critical to both operational and institutional gender mainstreaming are the people who bring this about. Feminist agents who work with organisations involved in the development process have been identified as essential in transforming the policy, planning, and implementation of development interventions (Goetz 1998, 2004; Porter and Judd 1999). These agents can be found in the vast majority of development organisations, regardless of whether the organisation is committed to gender mainstreaming of any kind. Sometimes these agents occupy posts which are not charged with supporting gender mainstreaming, but they are themselves feminists. Other agents with personal feminist commitment can be found in positions expressly charged with gender mainstreaming.

Feminist agents face a daily struggle to place and keep gender issues on the organisational agenda, with regard to both institutional practices and operational activities. Anne-Marie Goetz (2004) points to the need for more recognition and support for these agents to be given by their colleagues in the international women's movements. She also highlights the need for their work to be judged in context. Many changes brought about may not be immediately visible to those outside the organisation. Women's movements do not only have a role in supporting gender mainstreaming by pressuring and influencing from outside, but are also needed for alliance-building, solidarity, and support.

Feminist agents work alongside, and must influence, colleagues who may not identify themselves as feminists. Nevertheless, these colleagues have a key role to play in bringing about changes in development policy and practice. Development practitioners, particularly at the implementation level, are often the central actors in the success or failure of gender mainstreaming initiatives. A number of articles in this issue (including those of Senorina Wendoh and Tina Wallace, Kyoko Kusakabe, and Elsa Dawson) focus on the need for more attention to be paid to work with these actors. This work needs to recognise their location as individuals and as post holders, and to spend more time convincing them of the rationale for agenda-setting gender mainstreaming.

One insight from these articles is that at present there is a widespread over-reliance on two gender mainstreaming strategies: gender policy formulation, and gender training. In her article comparing gender mainstreaming policies in governments in three Asian countries, Kyoko Kusakabe provides examples of this. Gender policies are clearly an essential first step in mainstreaming, but, in themselves, they are insufficient to transform organisational practices, procedures, and structures. They can often seem imposed from above or outside. Without local-level adaptation, these policies can alienate the very people who are supposed to implement them. The result is passive or active resistance. Senorina Wendoh and Tina Wallace relate this problem to the current insistence of many international donors that gender inequality be addressed as part of funding agreements. Once the money is secured, although there might be a role such as 'gender adviser', this is often window dressing and little attention is paid to the need for policy formulation or subsequent activities to be shaped to local realities.

Gender training of development practitioners is often the only local-level activity to be included in funded inter-ventions. While gender training has potential to build commitment to put gender policies into practice, all too often the type of training offered fails to do this. Gender training, like gender policy formulation, is often not adapted to local realities. In addition, it has a tendency to focus narrowly on awareness raising, as if this will, in itself, enable individual practitioners to address gender inequality in their work. While gender awareness raising is critical, it often assumes a false homogeneity among women, failing to recognise other identities held by women and men which intersect with gender identity to create complex and unique experiences. The kind of training that is needed is very different. It would be tailored to the complex identities and lives of individual participants and communities, and would enable them to respond to specific opportunities and constraints for gender mainstreaming in their personal and professional contexts.

Rights-based approaches to development and gender mainstreaming

One factor which should facilitate a transformative approach to gender main-streaming is a political analysis of poverty and development. It has been argued that the empowerment of women as a concept should have a natural entrée into the concerns of organisations which are addressing the politics of inequality (Mayoux 1998). These may be political liberation movements, or 'alternative' development organisations (Riddell and Robinson 1995). These have an avowedly political perspective on poverty, and hence have an 'emphasis... not so much on service delivery or development programmes, but on organising the poor with a view to enabling them to exercise greater influence over decisions affecting their lives' (ibid., 35). However, such approaches often fail to discern difference within communities, including difference arising from gender inequality. Liberation struggles focus on overthrowing despotic governments and need the support of women as well as men to ensure success. The strategic gender interests of women tend to be sidelined while the struggle rages (Molyneux 1985), and often afterwards the new government fails to take them up (Molyneux 1991).

Shamim Meer's article in this issue demonstrates clearly the struggle of women to ensure that their shared interests were incorporated into the agenda of South Africa's post-apartheid government. However, this has resulted in what she calls a 'technicisation' of gender issues, which has marginalised women's collective political interests and stalled progress towards gender equality in South Africa. The energies of women activists-turned-politicians were often taken up with the business of government. Mainstream politics has not proved to be an effective forum in which to challenge gender inequality and promote women's rights. In matters like land reform, which affect both women and men, building in a gender analysis has met with resistance. Meanwhile, women's gender-specific concerns are still addressed, in the main, outside of government. The South African women's movement has successfully organised around issues such as abortion and violence against women.

Outside government, development organisations with a political analysis of poverty are faced with particular challenges when they start to address gender inequality. If development organisations base their vision and working practices on a commitment to ending unjust and unequal relations between the global North and South, analyses of gender inequality within Southern communities potentially weaken the power of this message. Added to this, such commitments to empowering marginal groups are not always genuine: populist approaches are not always radical approaches (Pieterse 1998), and gender equality is a radical aim. Elizabeth Harrison observes that 'development agencies are not in the business of promoting political realignments or supporting revolutionary struggles' (1995, 41). Aruna Rao and David Kelleher, in their article in this issue, suggest that development organisations contain within their 'deep structure' a conservatism reflecting their administrative and technical concerns, which should be uncovered and

examined in order to identify appropriate strategies for gender mainstreaming. This requires a political response, and an analysis of power, citizenship, and rights. This political response also needs to reflect an understanding of the added threat presented by right-wing populist agendas, which can actively undermine support for women's rights, while appealing to women as a political group.

Gender mainstreaming, men, and masculinity

Some contributions to this issue have made reference to the importance of masculinity to gender analysis, and to the importance of men in gender mainstreaming initiatives.

Considering masculinity as an issue in gender and development work is a logical outcome of changing terminology from WID to gender and development (GAD). For some, this outcome is not welcome. GAD set out to put a political edge on development targeted at women, and to emphasise the need to challenge inequality. But it has ended up being undermined by a focus on men's experience of gender relations, which threatens to divert attention from the global picture of continued female marginalisation from power at every level of society. Of course, local realities turn up examples of male powerlessness and poverty, in which the experience of particular men or boys is shaped by their gender identity. Gendered expectations of men can make extreme and appalling demands on individual men who cannot live up to what society expects of them. In such contexts, development organisations are presented with the choice to spend resources on addressing male gender issues. What is critical is that resources are not diverted from women, and that in addressing male gender issues, a commitment to gender equality remains non-negotiable.[2]

Men are also critically important as a constituency which can either make or break the success of gender mainstreaming.

In their article, Senorina Wendoh and Tina Wallace point out that in many contexts working with men, particularly powerful men in community leadership roles, is essential to the success of gender mainstreaming initiatives.

Conclusion: women subverting gender mainstreaming

Gender mainstreaming has, after ten years, had limited success. Integrationist approaches have not succeeded completely in their comparatively modest aim of addressing 'women's issues' within existing development agendas, while agenda-setting approaches have yet to be attempted in the vast majority of organisations.

Gender mainstreaming needs to be seen in perspective, as does planned development itself. Throughout history and across the world, women have used the opportunities they see to gain access to the resources they need. Development organisations can offer women the chance to obtain resources, which enable them to further practical or strategic interests of different kinds. This occurs regardless of the political intentions of the organisation.

However, development organisations should not be complacent, leaving it to women themselves to bring about changes in gender power relations. Gender equality is an intrinsic part of the vision of human development (Sen 1999). Development cannot be said to be just unless structural gender inequality is challenged and eradicated in all social, economic, and political institutions. Development organisations — both within and outside government — have a key role to play. They are important to individual women living in poverty as sources of money, information, and other essential commodities. They are also powerful voices in advocating for structural change to end discrimination against women as a sex. Gender mainstreaming can only be brought about by equal attention to the empowerment of women as agents of their own destiny, and structural gender equality.

Notes

1 The Beijing Platform for Action mentioned the term 'gender mainstreaming' over 35 times (AWID 2004).
2 Although some contributions do refer to the importance of men and masculinities, unfortunately we were unable to source contributions specifically addressing this issue. Please refer to past issues of this journal for relevant articles. In addition, readers with experience on this issue are invited to contact the editor to discuss possible contributions to a future issue on this topic.

References

Association for Women's Rights in Development (AWID) (2004) 'Gender mainstreaming: can it work for women's rights?', *Spotlight* 3, November

Cornwall, A. (2001) *Making a Difference? Gender and Participatory Development*, IDS Discussion Paper No. 378, Brighton: Institute of Development Studies

Elson, D. (1991), *Male Bias In the Development Process*, Manchester: University of Manchester

Goetz, A.M. (1998) *Getting Institutions Right for Women in Development*, London: Zed

Goetz, A.M. (2004) 'Reinvigorating autonomous feminist spaces', *IDS Bulletin*, 35(4): 137-140

Harrison, E. (1995) 'Fish and feminists', *IDS Bulletin* 26(3): 39-48

Jahan, R. (1995) *The Elusive Agenda: Mainstreaming Women in Development* London: Zed

Kabeer, N, (1999), 'Resources, agency, achievements: reflections on the measurement of women's empowerment', *Development and Change* Vol. 30, pp. 435-64

Kardam, N. (1993) 'Development approaches and the role of policy advocacy: the case of the World Bank', *World Development* 21(11) pp.773-86

Mayoux, L. (1998) 'Gender accountability and NGOs: avoiding the black hole', in C. Miller and S. Razavi (eds.) *Missionaries and Mandarins: Feminist Engagement With Development Institutions*, London: Intermediate Technology Development Group

Miller, C. (1998) 'Gender advocates and multilateral development organisations: promoting change from within', in C. Miller and S. Razavi (eds.) *Missionaries and Mandarins: Feminist Engagement With Development Institutions*, London: Intermediate Technology Development Group

Molyneux, M. (1985). 'Mobilisation without emancipation? Women's interests, the state and revolution in Nicaragua', *Feminist Studies* 11(2), pp. 227-53

Molyneux M. (1991) 'The "woman question" in the age of perestroika', in R. Blackburn (ed.) *After the Fall*, London: Verso

Moser, C. (1989) 'Gender planning in the Third World: meeting practical and strategic gender needs', *World Development* 17(11) pp. 1799–825

Pearson, R. (1999) 'Rethinking gender matters in development', in T. Allen and A. Thomas (eds.) *Poverty and Development in the 1990s*, Milton Keynes: Open University

Pieterse, J.N. (1998) 'My paradigm or yours? Alternative development, post-development, reflexive development', *Development and Change* 29:343-73

Porter, M. (1999) 'Introduction: Caught in the web?' in M. Porter and E. Judd (eds.) (1999)

Porter, M. and Judd, E. (eds.) (1999) *Feminists Doing Development: A Practical Critique*, Zed: London

Rao, A. Stuart, R., and Kelleher, D. (1999) *Gender at Work*, Bloomfield: Kumarian

Riddell, R.C. and Robinson, M. (1995) *Non-governmental Organisations and Rural Poverty Alleviation*, Oxford: Oxford University Press/Clarendon Press

Sen, A. (1999) *Development as Freedom*, Oxford: Oxford University Press

United Nations (1997) 'Report of the Economic and Social Council for 1997', A/52/3, 18 September 1997

Young, K. (1993) *Development Planning with Women: Making a World of Difference*, New York: St Martin's Press

Gender mainstreaming since Beijing:
a review of success and limitations in international institutions

Caroline Moser and Annalise Moser

The Beijing Platform for Action prioritised gender mainstreaming as the mechanism to achieve gender equality. A decade later, policy makers and practitioners are debating whether this has succeeded or failed. This article aims to contribute to this debate by reviewing progress made to date, through a review of gender mainstreaming policies in international development institutions. Categorising progress into three stages — adoption of terminology, putting a policy into place, and implementation — the article argues that while most institutions have put gender mainstreaming policies in place, implementation remains inconsistent. Most important of all, the outcomes and impact of the implementation of gender mainstreaming in terms of gender equality remain largely unknown, with implications for the next decade's strategies.

In 1995, governments across the world signed the Beijing Platform for Action. Along with their endorsement of the Plan of Action went a commitment to achieve 'gender equality and the empowerment of women'. Gender mainstreaming (defined in the next section) was identified as the most important mechanism to reach this ambitious goal. Throughout the process, international institutions have provided a variety of support to governments and civil society alike, be it analytical, institutional, or financial in nature.

A decade after the UN Conference on Women, held in Beijing, practitioners around the world are asking if gender mainstreaming has succeeded, while some sceptics are already talking of its 'failure'. This calls for a stocktaking of progress to date. What have been the experiences of gender mainstreaming? Has the enormous range and diversity of activities ultimately had an impact on gender equality on the ground? Are gender training methodologies appropriate today, and are measurement indicators sufficient? It is now an appropriate moment to address these and other critical issues relating to gender mainstreaming.

This is no easy task. The purpose of this article is to begin to tackle this issue through a review of the gender mainstreaming policies of international institutions. It provides an assessment of progress to date in 14 international development institutions or organisations, including bilateral donors, international financial institutions (IFIs), United Nations (UN) agencies, and non-government organisations (NGOs).[1] The review categorises progress in gender mainstreaming in terms of the following three stages:

- adopting the terminology of gender equality and gender mainstreaming;

- putting a gender mainstreaming policy into place;

- implementing gender mainstreaming.

This provides the basis for a synthesis of progress, and the identification of limitations and gaps. It is hoped that these, in turn, will contribute to the development of new strategies for gender mainstreaming in the next decade.

Adopting the terminology of gender equality and gender mainstreaming

At the international level, most development institutions have adopted the terminology of gender equality and gender mainstreaming, and are relatively consistent in its use. Among those that define gender equality, there is a general consensus that it refers to the recognition that women and men have different needs and priorities, and that women and men should 'experience equal conditions for realising their full human rights, and have the opportunity to contribute to and benefit from national, political, economic, social and cultural development' (CIDA 1999).

Most definitions of gender mainstreaming across institutions adhere closely to those set out by the UN Economic and Social Council (UN 1997, 28) as follows:

> *Mainstreaming a gender perspective is the process of assessing the implications for women and men of any planned action, including legislation, policies or programmes, in all areas and at all levels. It is a strategy for making women's as well as men's concerns and experiences an integral dimension of the design, implementation, monitoring and evaluation of policies and programmes in all political, economic and societal spheres so that women and men benefit equally and inequality is not perpetuated. The ultimate goal is to achieve gender equality.*

In addition, two further aspects of gender mainstreaming appear in some definitions, namely:

- *the institutionalisation of gender concerns within the organisation itself:* relating to taking account of gender equality in administrative, financial, staffing, and other organisational procedures, thus contributing to a long-term transformative process for the organisation in terms of attitudes, 'culture', goals, and procedures;

- *gender empowerment:* promoting women's participation in decision-making processes, as well as having their voices heard and the power to put issues on the agenda.

Putting in place a gender mainstreaming policy[2]

In the past decade, the majority of major development institutions have developed and endorsed a gender policy.[3] Indeed, all those included in this review have endorsed such a policy.

Components of gender mainstreaming policy

The majority of such gender mainstreaming policies share the following six key components, as summarised in Table 1:

- a dual strategy of mainstreaming gender combined with targeted actions for gender equality;

- gender analysis;

- a combined approach to responsibilities, where all staff share responsibility, but are supported by gender specialists;

- gender training;

- support to women's decision making and empowerment;

- monitoring and evaluation.

Three additional components — working with other organisations, budgets, and knowledge resources — are shared by a smaller number of institutions.

Table 1. Components and associated activities of gender mainstreaming policy[4]

Components	Activities	Bilaterals			IFIs			UN System				NGOs				%
		DFID	CIDA	Sida	IDB	Asian DB	WB	UNIFEM	Habitat	UNICEF	UNDP	ActionAid	Oxfam GB	Hivos	ACORD	
Dual strategy of mainstreaming and targeting gender equality	Mainstreaming into policies, projects and programmes (all stages of cycle)	X	X	X	X	X	X	X	X	X	X	X	X	X	X	100
	Actions targeting gender equality	X	X	X	X	X	X	X	X	X	X	X	X	X	X	100
Gender analysis	Sex-disaggregated data and gender info	X	X		X			X	X		X					43
	Analysis at all programme cycle stages	X	X	X	X	X	X	X	X			X	X		X	79
	Gender sensitive budget analysis										X					7
Internal responsibility	Responsibilities shared between all staff and gender specialists/focal points	X	X	X			X	X	X	X	X	X	X	X	X	79
Gender Training	Understanding and implementation of gender policy for staff and counterparts	X		X								X	X	X	X	43
	Staff/counterpart gender sensitisation												X			7
	Staff/counterpart gender training/skills	X	X		X	X	X	X	X	X	X	X	X	X	X	93
	Manuals, tool kits	X				X	X	X	X	X						43
Support to women's decision making and empowerment	Strengthening women's organisations through capacity building and training		X			X		X				X	X	X		36
	Support to women's participation in decision making/empowerment	X	X	X	X			X	X	X	X	X	X	X	X	86
	Working with men for gender equality		X	X							X		X	X	X	43
Monitoring and evaluation	Effective systems and tools for M&E	X	X	X	X	X	X		X	X	X	X	X	X	X	93
	Gender-sensitive indicators								X			X				14
Work with other organisations	Strengthening gender equality in work with government, donors, UN, private sector and NGOs			X	X	X	X	X				X	X	X	X	71
	Capacity building of civil society	X	X	X				X	X		X					43
	Support to national women's machineries		X	X				X								21
Budgets	Allocation of financial resources for staff to carry out gender policy	X			X		X	X				X	X		X	50
Knowledge resources	Publications/knowledge base on best practice and effective strategies				X	X	X	X			X		X		X	50
	Networks		X					X			X					21
	Online data bases							X			X					14

Source: DFID (2000); Derbyshire (2002); CIDA (1999); Sida (1997); IDB (n.d.); ADB (1998); World Bank (2002); Sandler (1997); UN Habitat (2002); UNICEF (2000); UNDP (2002); ActionAid (2000); Oxfam GB (1993); Hivos (1996); ACORD (1999).

Most importantly, all organisations identify a dual strategy of mainstreaming gender equality issues into all policies, programmes and projects, combined with supporting targeted actions for gender equality (100 per cent). The majority mention the need for gender training (93 per cent), and for systems and tools for monitoring and evaluation (93 per cent). Some form of gender analysis is identified by 86 per cent, as is support for women's active role in decision-making processes and empowerment — mentioned by all except the World Bank and the Asian Development Bank (ADB). Finally, the issue of the responsibility for gender mainstreaming shows a combined approach, where all staff share responsibility, but are supported by gender specialists. Exceptions to this approach include the Inter-American Development Bank (IDB) and ADB, and the UN agencies dedicated to gender. Institutionally, gender specialists are often located within a centralised team, as well as 'embedded' in decentralised departmental and regional offices. In an assessment of the NGO Hivos, Dubel (2002) notes that this structure allows for top–down (policy development and programmatic support) and bottom–up (policy operationalisation) processes.

Other gender mainstreaming components less frequently cited include the need to identify the roles and responsibilities of staff (57 per cent), and strengthening gender equality in co-operation with other organisations (71 per cent). Half mentioned the generation and distribution of best-practice publications, as well as attention to the allocation of adequate resources. Just under half also cited capacity building of civil society, and learning through manuals and tool kits, as being important to gender mainstreaming strategies.

Among types of institutions, minimal differences are apparent. Bilateral organisations report more activities concerned with strengthening civil society and working with national women's machineries. UN agencies make use of networks and online data bases to disseminate knowledge, and have an extensive system of gender focal points within each agency. The UN is also unique in that it has several agencies or divisions dedicated to gender equality — including UNIFEM, the Division for the Advancement of Women (DAW), and the Inter-Agency Network on Women and Gender Equality (IANWGE) — which provide support and co-ordination for the UN system. These last two entities were not included in Table 1, as they are not stand-alone operational agencies. They provide support for gender activities in other UN agencies, particularly through supporting gender equality in co-operation with other organisations, and providing a range of knowledge resources.

Policy constraints: the problem of instrumentalism

Although all institutions in this review have succeeded in developing an explicit gender policy, evaluations highlight as a constraint the issue of instrumentalism. Since gender policy is generally formulated within a particular organisational context, with specific pressures, mandate and ideology, the gender policy and the organisational mandate need to 'fit' (Razavi 1997). Here the debate concerns the extent to which gender equality policy should be developed as an end in itself or, as advocates of instrumentalism argue, promoted as a means to development. In this case poverty reduction is most frequently utilised as a useful platform. Advocates argue that this promotes a win–win scenario, as in the 1995 Human Development Report phrase 'development, if not engendered, is endangered' (UNDP 1995).

Three main arguments are used to defend instrumentalism. First, it may be inevitable, given the constraints of the contexts within which feminist advocates operate. Second, in the 'real' world of politics, compromises and strategic alliances are parts of reality. Finally, instrumentalism can be a way of subverting neo-liberal discourse. Nevertheless, critics of an instrumental gender engagement strategy argue that it risks depoliticising the transformative nature of the feminist agenda (Miller and Razavi 1998), and presents problems when there are conflicts between gender policy and other issues.

Implementing gender mainstreaming

It is clear that most international development institutions have put in place gender mainstreaming policies. Therefore, it is at the level of implementation that significant challenges remain. As Heyzer (quoted in Valk 2000) notes,

Through regional and international conferences, we have achieved far-reaching agreements on gender equality. The challenge now is holding stakeholders —governments, UN agencies, the private sector, and civil society — accountable for implementation.

Turning to the implementation of gender mainstreaming, most efforts are considered inconsistent, and generally involve only a few activities, rather than a coherent and integrated process. Sida, for instance, found that interventions showed only 'embryonic evidence' of working with gender mainstreaming processes (Mikkelsen et al. 2002). Similar 'patchy' efforts towards gender mainstreaming were identified by Danida (2000), UNDP (Schalkwyk 1998), and two reviews of NGOs (Wallace 1998; Mayoux 1998).

Policy commitments to gender mainstreaming frequently evaporate in planning and implementation processes. An NGO evaluation of DFID explicitly identified this as a constraint (MacDonald 2003; see also Longwe 1995; Derbyshire 2002). When this occurs, high-level commitments are not reflected in country or sectoral policies, and the overall gender policy commitment becomes less visible in the process of specifying project objectives, results, and evaluations (DAC 1998). The problem of policy evaporation can be due a number of factors. These include lack of staff capacity (exacerbated by the frequent use of — junior — consultants); organisational culture and attitudes, including resistance to the notion of gender equality; the treatment of gender equality as a separate process, which marginalises rather than mainstreams the issue; staff 'simplification' of the gender issue; and a lack of feeling of ownership of the policy (DAC 1998; Derbyshire 2002; Valk 2000).

However, as UNIFEM emphasises (Sandler 1997), ultimately gender mainstreaming is a process rather than a goal. Therefore, it may not make sense to argue that mainstreaming has failed. Rather, it is important to identify which aspects of gender mainstreaming are in place within organisations, and which are the overall constraints to implementing a comprehensive strategy. Implementation comprises both institutional and operational inputs, with the two closely interrelated. The outputs and outcomes/impacts of implementation are measured in terms of greater gender equality (Moser 1995). Table 2 summarises these in terms of constraints identified in this review as well as identifying data limitations. This shows that, to date, assessments have focused more on institutional inputs than those relating to the process of operational and programming implementation. Finally the outcomes and impact of implementation in terms of gender equality still require far more attention. The following section elaborates on the constraints identified in relation to each of these inputs.

Table 2. Implementation of gender mainstreaming policy

Implementation input	Constraints	Evaluations of implementation, outcomes, and data limitations
Institutional	internal responsibility organisational culture resistance mechanisms for accountability gender training	Extensive evaluation of implementation of institutional components shows that significant challenges remain.
Operational	need for monitoring and evaluation dilemmas with participation	Very few evaluations are available that address operational outcomes and impact on gender equality.

Institutional inputs

The majority of gender mainstreaming evaluations focus on institutional inputs, with attention from NGOs, bilateral agencies, and UN agencies, as well as more general assessments. These raise a range of constraints including the following.

Internal responsibility

Although most organisations have promoted a combined approach, where all staff share responsibility but are supported by gender specialists, success in gender mainstreaming is still highly reliant on the commitment and skills of *key individuals*, as identified for example in Hivos, DFID, and Sida (Hivos 2001; MacDonald 2003; Mikkelsen *et al.* 2002). In the UK, for instance, NGOs with gender specialists have made the most progress on gender issues (Wallace 1998). At the same time, when gender mainstreaming is the responsibility of all staff, gender issues can be diluted or disappear altogether, through non-committed decision makers and male resistance, while specialised gender focal points can be marginalised from mainstream activities (March *et al.* 1999). Equally a gender unit at head office can be regarded by field staff as top–down or culturally coercive (Wallace 1998).

Organisational culture

Programme success on gender equality and organisational culture are intrinsically linked; as Oxfam staff asked, 'could we realistically expect to achieve at the programme-level what we could not achieve in our own workplace?' (Oxfam 2003). An organisational culture which is male-biased, in terms of attitudes, recruitment, working conditions, and structures and procedures, 'discriminates against female staff and clients' (Valk 2000). Organisational culture was mentioned as a constraint by NGOs such as Oxfam, ActionAid Nepal, and those studied by Wallace, as well as UNDP, DFID, and Eurostep agencies (Oxfam 2003; Rai 2000; Wallace 1998; Schalkwyk 1998; MacDonald 2003; MacDonald et al. 1997).

A study of the 'deep structures' of organisations identified how gender inequality is perpetuated through the valorisation of heroic individualism; the split between work and family; exclusionary power; and the 'monoculture of instrumentality' (Rao and Kelleher 2002). Many organisations still have male-dominated senior management, directors, and trustees, and gender commitments in job descriptions are not rigorously pursued (Wallace 1998). In DFID, for example, the target of having women in 30 per cent of senior civil servant posts is far from being met (MacDonald 2003). In ActionAid Nepal, the gender imbalance was so severe that they introduced a temporary women-only recruitment policy, which raised the percentage of women staff from 12 per cent to 24 per cent (Rai 2000). Male-biased organisational culture can also exclude women through the scarcity of high-level job shares, extensive travel requirements, and long work hours, all of which are difficult for women with dependent children (Wallace 1998).

Resistance

Closely linked to organisational culture is the issue of (usually male) resistance. Staff working on gender issues were faced by resistance from senior management through to field staff, as well as 'cultural resistance' noted by ACORD and Eurostep agencies (Hadjipateras 1997; MacDonald *et al.* 1997). In Sida, it was found that resistance can come from conservative interests at the political and institutional levels, as well as from men at the institutional level (Mikkelsen *et al.* 2002). At the UNDP, gender focal points recognised both active and passive forms of resistance (Schalkwyk 1998). Some sectors and countries provide more resistance than others (Danida 2000). This evidence suggests a need for work on transforming attitudes, and for training.

Mechanisms for accountability

There is a widely acknowledged need for *specific* mechanisms of accountability, rather than simply the general guidelines provided in policy statements. These include *incentives* for positive behaviour as well as appropriate *sanctions* (Wallace 1998; Hivos 2001; UN Inter-Agency Meeting on Women and Gender Equality [UNIAMWGE] 2001; CIDA 2000; Rao and Friedman 2000). Related to this is the fact that gender experts, including focal points, advisers and others, are often junior staff and/or consultants who have little power to influence or advise (see Schalkwyk 1998).

There are few specific guidelines or requirements, such as minimum standards, in order to move beyond the deterrence of an all-or-nothing approach, and few specific gender equality goals and targets in programme or project planning and design (Mikkelsen *et al.* 2002; Hadjipateras 1997). There has also been a call for systems of monitoring and evaluation to be applied to organisation-level issues (Rai 2000; MacDonald *et al.* 1997). MacDonald *et al.* (1997) provide a potential gender assessment framework for an organisation, addressing mission and goal; strategy; products; structure; operations; decision making; planning, monitoring, and evaluation; communication; personnel; resources; organisational culture; and external context.

Gender training

Interestingly, there was a consistently reported need for further and improved gender training at all levels. This was due to resistance and negative attitudes towards gender issues, and to a lack of staff understanding about basic concepts, the relevance to their work, and how to mainstream gender into their work. These was identified for example by Oxfam, ACORD, and DFID (Oxfam 2003; Hadjipateras 1997; MacDonald 2003). While training had been provided in the past, a high turnover of staff has meant that at any given point, many staff members have never received gender training.

Gender training therefore needs to be not a one-off event, but ongoing and consistently refreshed. It needs to be made more specific or tailored to operational activities, clearly demonstrating its relevance to the work that people do. There needs to be follow-up in terms of 'trying out' the new skills. Gender training also needs to be more culturally sensitive (Wallace 1998), with South–South training encouraged.

Operational /programming outcomes and impact on gender equality

The review revealed far fewer assessments of operational aspects of gender mainstreaming, including outcomes and impacts on gender equality — the ultimate goal of gender mainstreaming (see DAC 1998). The following constraints in particular were identified.

Monitoring and evaluation

The most commonly cited constraint at the operational level was the lack of effective, consistent, and systematic monitoring and evaluation of gender mainstreaming outcomes and impacts. This was mentioned by Sida (Mikkelsen *et al.* 2002), Danida (2000), DAC (1998), Hivos (2001), UNIAMWGE (2001), ACORD (Hadjipateras 1997), Wallace (1998), and Mayoux (1998). This lack of evaluation means that it is difficult to know the effects of gender mainstreaming on gender equality and people's lives; as UNIAMWGE (2001) notes, there is a need to link strategies with concrete outcomes.

One of the challenges here involves identifying criteria for assessment, including appropriate indicators. Assessments often focus on input indicators such as the number and proportion of female beneficiaries, and number of activities, rather than addressing impacts or outcomes (Mayoux 1998; Hadjipateras 1997). The development of indicators on gender concerns presents several challenges. One is the need for uniform criteria, determined by consensus. Another is the difficulty of measuring changes in power and status. Such challenges make impact assessment a lengthy, difficult, and costly process.

Some of the recent work in this field has concerned indicators of empowerment. A comprehensive study by Malhorta, Schuler, and Boender (2003) employs Kabeer's (2001) definition of empowerment ('the expansion in people's ability to make strategic life choices in a context where this ability was previously denied to them'). The study synthesises a range of indicators used to measure women's empowerment. While these relate to women's empowerment in general terms, rather than as an outcome of specific development interventions, the study raises some interesting issues such as the need for multiple indicators and triangulation, and combining qualitative and quantitative indicators. They suggest that women's empowerment needs to occur along six different dimensions: economic, socio-cultural, familial/interpersonal, legal, political, and psychological. Each of these

should be measured at various levels of social aggregation, from the household, to the community, to broader national, regional, and global levels. For example, in the economic dimension, indicators of empowerment can include women's control over household income; their access to employment, credit, and markets; their representation in high-paying jobs; and representation of their interests in macro-economic policies.

One of the few impact assessments was from Sida (Mikkelsen *et al.* 2002). It evaluated the effects of interventions on gender equality in terms of the following criteria: practical gender needs and strategic gender changes; women's empowerment; and men, male roles, and masculinities. Findings included the fact that all but two interventions addressed practical gender needs, and these in turn contributed to strategic gender changes. Empowerment was rarely an explicit aim, but was a side effect in some interventions.

In terms of successful strategies for promoting outcomes for gender equality, Sida (Mikkelsen *et al.* 2002) has identified the following:

- Increased participation and access to resources contribute to practical gender needs.

- Visible and specific gender equality goals contribute to strategic gender needs.

- The possibility of positive changes are increased when there is flexible programme design and development, with goals and targets being implemented during the life of the programme.

- Ownership of gender equality by the host institution is important.

- Participatory approaches and dialogue are needed.

ACORD (Hadjipateras 1997) used the Longwe framework to assess impact on gender equality in terms of welfare, access to resources, conscientisation, participation, and control. The greatest gains for women overall were in the spheres of welfare, access to resources, conscientisation, and to a lesser extent participation. There was limited impact on the 'ultimate level' of control. Other indicators include participation in decision making, and men and women benefiting equally, used by Oxfam in Sierra Leone (2003); and practical gender needs and an increase in equality of opportunity, influence, and benefit, suggested by DFID (Derbyshire 2002). At the macro level, composite indicators measure gender equality, for example, the Millennium Development Goals' indicators, and the Gender-Related Development Index.

Women's participation

There are important dilemmas inherent in promoting women's participation. As both DAC (1998) and UNIFEM (Sandler 1997) state, gender mainstreaming should not be concerned with simply increasing women's participation, but with the *terms* of their participation. Increasing women's participation is not always beneficial for women. Many NGOs show a bias towards mobilisation of women's unpaid labour as an example of women's participation, often yielding negligible benefits for women and using their time (Moser 1993). Evidence also suggests that participation is often limited to the formation of participatory groups at the local level in specific projects determined from the outside. Grassroots constituencies have little influence over decision making at other levels of the organisation (*ibid.*).

Cornwall (2003) argues that while the ethics of gender and development, and of participatory development, concern challenging and changing relations of power and agency, in practice they can simply exacerbate existing exclusion and unequal gender roles. Requiring that women are represented or consulted is necessary but not sufficient: are their voices actually heard? Is the participation of a particular woman representative of women in general?

Does their presence simply legitimise decisions made by men? What if women make decisions that appear to reinforce their subordination? What of the differences among women? Whether and how gender issues are raised in participatory processes often depends on the agency, assumptions, and understandings of those who shape the process, whether field researchers or policy makers.

Guijt and Shah (1998) argue that the use of 'community' as a unit of analysis or intervention has often led to social hierarchies and gender differences being overlooked. Here issues of power can be forgotten, and empowerment simplified to raising issues with local people, but not following through with transformative strategies: a process which is ultimately not empowering. To address these issues within gender and participation, three areas of attention are called for: conceptual clarity, appropriate and consistent methodologies, and organisational support and institutional consistency.

Conclusions

There is still no consensus on the failure or success of gender mainstreaming at the international level, with documentation in the public domain both fragmented and arbitrary. What is clear is that, for the most part, international institutions have put in place gender mainstreaming policies. In terms of the implementation of those policies, however, the evidence is mixed. The majority of evaluations have concerned institutional inputs, with varying successes and limitations identified. By contrast, very few assessments have addressed the operational and programming implementation of gender mainstreaming. Above all, the outcomes and impact of implementation in terms of gender equality are still largely unknown. Thus, the next decade calls for a twofold strategy: implementation of gender mainstreaming (with far greater transparency in terms of documentation), and the development of more robust evaluations of output and outcome processes. So while progress has been made, the next decade will provide the real test of gender mainstreaming in practice.

Caroline Moser is a social anthropology/social policy researcher affiliated to ODI, London and Brookings Institution, Washington DC. Current research includes intergenerational asset building and poverty reduction strategies, with fieldwork in Ecuador; women's organizations in peace processes with capacity strengthening in Colombia; and gender mainstreaming audits in the Beijing plus 10 context.
Address: 4841 Albemarle Street NW, Washington DC 20016, USA.
Email: carolinemoser44@aol.com

Annalise Moser is a Programme Specialist with UNIFEM, working on gender and conflict prevention in the Solomon Islands. She has a PhD in social anthropology, and has worked as a consultant on women and peacebuilding, human rights and gender-based violence. Address: UNIFEM, C/ PO Box 1954, Honiara, SOLOMON ISLANDS.
Email: annalisemoser@hotmail.com

Notes

1 A systematic analysis was conducted of the following organisations: DFID (UK Department for International Development), CIDA (Canadian International Development Agency), Sida (Swedish International Development Agency), the World Bank, the IDB (Inter-American Development Bank), the ADB (Asian Development Bank), UNICEF (United Nations Children's Fund), UNDP (United Nations Development Programme), UN Habitat, UNIFEM (United Nations Development Fund for Women), Oxfam GB, Hivos (Humanitarian Institute for Development Cooperation), ActionAid, and ACORD (Agency for Cooperation and Research in Development). The background review relied entirely on available documentation. The absence of a particular concept or component does not necessarily mean that it does not exist within the organisation, but that it was not mentioned in the documentation.

2 This review distinguishes between a policy as the statement of intended commitment and action, and a strategy as the range of activities or measures designed to ensure the implementation of a policy. It is necessary to note that many organisations do not make such a clear distinction, using the terms interchangeably.

3 Not all international institutions have such a policy. One study (Wallace 1998) found that only four of 17 UK NGOs had incorporated gender awareness into policies and procedures.

4 As specified in particular gender mainstreaming policies and strategies.

References

ACORD (1999) 'Gender Equality: Policy, Good Practice Guidelines and Action Plan for ACORD 2000-2003', London: ACORD

ActionAid (2000) 'Gender Policy', London: ActionAid

ADB (1998) 'Policy of Gender and Development', Manila: ADB

CIDA (1999) 'CIDA's Policy of Gender Equality', Hull, Quebec: CIDA

CIDA (2000) 'Accelerating Change: Resources for Gender Mainstreaming', Hull, Quebec: CIDA

Cornwall, A. (2003) 'Whose voices? Whose choices? Reflections on gender and participatory development', *World Development* 31(8): 1325-42

DAC (1998) 'DAC Source Book on Concepts and Approaches Linked to Gender Equality', Paris: OECD

Danida (2000) 'Gender Equality in Danish Development Co-operation: A Contribution to the Revision of Danish Development Policy', Copenhagen: Danida

Derbyshire, H. (2002) 'Gender Manual: A Practical Guide for Development Policy Makers and Practitioners', London: DFID

DFID (2000) *Poverty Elimination and the Empowerment of Women: Strategies for Achieving the International Development Targets*, London: DFID

Dubel, I. (2002) 'Challenges for Gender Mainstreaming – The Experiences of Hivos', paper presented at Women's Worlds 2002, Kampala, 21–26 July 2002

Guijt, I. and M.K. Shah (eds.) (1998) *The Myth of Community: Gender Issues in Participatory Development*, London: Intermediate Technology Publications

Hadjipateras, A. (1997) 'Implementing a gender policy in ACORD: strategies, constraints, and challenges', *Gender and Development* 5(1): 28-34

Hivos (1996) 'Hivos Policy Document: Gender, Women and Development', The Hague: Hivos

Hivos (2001) 'Report Gender Self-Assessment of Hivos Gender, Women and Development Policy (1997-2000)', The Hague: Hivos

IDB (n.d.) 'OP-761 Women in Development', Operational Policy, Washington, DC: IDB

Kabeer, N. (2001) 'Reflections on the measurement of women's empowerment', in *Discussing Women's Empowerment: Theory and Practice*, Sida Studies No. 3. Stockholm: Novum Grafiska AB

Longwe, S. (1995) 'The evaporation of policies for women's advancement', in N. Heyzer (ed) *A Commitment to the World's Women: Perspectives on Development for Beijing and Beyond*, New York: UNIFEM

MacDonald, M. (2003) 'Gender Equality and Mainstreaming in the Policy and Practice of the UK Department for International Development', London: Womankind

MacDonald, M., E. Sprenger and I. Dubel (1997) *Gender and Organizational Change: Bridging the Gap between Policy and Practice*, Amsterdam: Royal Tropical Institute

Malhotra, A., S. Schuler and C. Boender (2003) 'Measuring Women's Empowerment as a Variable in International Development', paper presented at the ICRW Insight and Action Seminar, Washington, DC, 12 November 2003

March, C., I. Smyth and M. Mukhopadhyay (1999) *A Guide to Gender-Analysis Frameworks*, Oxford: Oxfam GB

Mayoux, L. (1998) 'Gender accountability and NGOs: avoiding the black hole', in C. Miller and S. Razavi (eds.) *Missionaries and Mandarins: Feminist Engagement with Development Institutions*, London: Intermediate Technology

Mikkelsen, B., Freeman T., and Keller B. (2002) 'Mainstreaming Gender Equality: Sida's Support for the Promotion of Gender Equality in Partner Countries', Stockholm: Sida

Miller, C. and S. Razavi (1998) 'Introduction', in C. Miller and S. Razavi (eds.) *Missionaries and Mandarins: Feminist Engagement with Development Institutions*, London: Intermediate Technology

Moser, C. (1993) *Gender Planning and Development: Theory, Practice and Training*, London: Routledge

Moser, C. (1995) 'Evaluating gender impacts', *New Directions For Evaluation* 67(Fall): 105-118

Oxfam GB (1993) 'Oxfam GAD Policy,' Oxford: Oxfam

Oxfam (2003) *Links* May 2003

Rai, S. (2000) 'Gender and ActionAid Nepal', in H. van Dam, A. Khadar and M. Valk (eds.) *Institutionalising Gender Equality: Commitment, Policy and Practice, A Global Sourcebook*, KIT Publishers and Oxfam GB: Netherlands and Oxford

Rao, A. and Friedman, M. (2000) 'Transforming institutions: history and challenges: an international perspective', in H. van Dam, A. Khadar and M. Valk (eds.) *Institutionalising Gender Equality: Commitment, Policy and Practice, A Global Sourcebook*, Netherlands and Oxford: KIT Publishers and Oxfam GB

Rao, A. and D. Kelleher (2002) 'Unravelling Institutionalised Gender Inequality', Occasional Paper Number 8, AWID

Razavi, S. (1997) 'Fitting gender into development institutions', *World Development* 25(7): 1111-26

Sandler, J. (1997) 'UNIFEM's Experiences in Mainstreaming for Gender Equality', New York: UNIFEM

Schalkwyk, J. (1998) 'Building Capacity for Gender Mainstreaming: UNDP's Experience', New York: UNDP

Sida, (1997) 'Sida's Action Program for Promoting Equality between Women and Men in Partner Countries: Policy, Experience Analysis, Action Plan', Stockholm: Sida

United Nations (1997) 'Report of the Economic and Social Council for 1997', A/52/3, 18 September 1997

UNDP (1995) *Human Development Report,* Oxford: Oxford University Press

UNDP (2002) 'Gender Equality: Practice Note', New York: UNDP

UN Habitat (2002) 'Habitat's Gender Policy', Kenya: UN Habitat

UNICEF (2000) 'Equality, Development and Peace', New York: UNICEF

UN Inter-Agency Meeting on Women and Gender Equality (2001) 'Report: Workshop on Approaches and Methodologies for Gender Mainstreaming', New York, 27 February–2 March 2001

Valk, M. (2000) 'Introduction: commitments to women and gender', in H. van Dam, A. Khadar and M. Valk (eds.) *Institutionalising Gender Equality: Commitment, Policy and Practice, A Global Sourcebook*, Netherlands and Oxford: KIT Publishers and Oxfam GB

Wallace, T. (1998) 'Institutionalising gender in UK NGOs', *Development in Practice* 8(2): 159-72

World Bank (2002) 'Integrating Gender into the World Bank's Work: A Strategy for Action', Washington, DC: World Bank

Gender mainstreaming or just more male-streaming?
Experiences of popular participation in Bolivia

Suzanne Clisby

The Law of Popular Participation (LPP) in Bolivia can be seen as the first significant attempt by policy makers in the region to mainstream gender into a national development initiative. The LPP seeks to devolve power and resources from the national to the local level. It is the first Bolivian law to be explicitly couched in gendered terms, and aims to increase the prominence of women in local political and development spheres. However, as I suggest in this article, in some respects the LPP has actually had the effect of displacing women from the very site of their traditional forms of political activism, at community level. As greater status, power, and resources have been devolved to politics at this level, men have become more prominent in this previously neglected, 'feminised' sphere. The article argues that, to some extent, the goal of mainstreaming gender into national development via the LPP was missed. Reasons include a lack of effective and systematic gendered analysis of the structural barriers to women's participation, and the failure to support gender mainstreaming, and women's participation, through capacity building at all levels.

The term 'gender mainstreaming' has become common parlance in development policy documents in recent years. The Fourth World Conference on Women in Beijing in 1995 was a critical forum at which a commitment to integrating a gender perspective in all forms of development and political processes was drawn up in the Platform for Action (PfA) (United Nations 2001). This commitment to an integration of a gendered perspective at all levels subsequently became labelled *gender mainstreaming*. It has become a major global strategy for ensuring the incorporation of gender perspectives and the promotion of gender equality in all areas of social development (Neimanis 2003).

However, much more work still needs to be done to translate the policy rhetoric into grounded reality. Indeed, unless gender mainstreaming is genuinely translated from rhetoric to reality, there is a danger that it

becomes little more than fashionable semantics co-opted by politicians and policy makers, and that women will actually lose out in the longer term. When terminology becomes accepted at a policy level without the corresponding implementation and structural transformation, it can serve to blunt demands, in this case women's demands, for change. It can also elicit responses along the lines of, 'we've done that, it's been dealt with, you no longer have legitimate grounds for complaint'.

With this in mind, this article provides a critical analysis of an attempt to mainstream gender into a potentially radical political reform that has been rolled out across Bolivia since the mid-1990s. The LPP — also known as the People's Participation Law, or Law 1551 — has attracted significant international attention and is generally heralded as a groundbreaking force for enhanced citizenship, democratisation, and much-needed community development. Indeed, over the past decade there has been a tangible sense of both increased empowerment and of greater enfranchisement into regional and national political processes among local actors (Imparato and Ruster 2003; Byron and Zolezzi 2003; Booth and Piron 2004).

Nevertheless, in all the excitement that the LPP has generated about people's participation, far less attention has been paid to the actual gendered dynamics of the law. As I suggest here, the LPP fell short of its potential to effectively mainstream gender into the political processes, for two key reasons. First, there was a lack of attention paid to gendered analyses of both practical and strategic[1] barriers to women's participation at the policy level. Second, there was a failure to provide adequate and systematic capacity building to facilitate women's participation at local and regional levels. As a result, rather than encouraging women's greater participation and decision making, the LPP has in some cases had the reverse effect of pushing women out of local spaces in which they were previously involved in community development. Moreover, as Lind (2002) states, since the popular participation measures were introduced, the percentage of women politicians and in some cases of women's organisational participation has actually decreased. In addition, she argues,

> even when women's organizations participate in these new structures, they may gain visibility but they do not necessarily gain political or economic power. An unintended consequence of decentralization is that some women's organizations have lost out or been left without funding or support (Lind 2002, 242).

While there is some evidence that this may be a transitional phase, and one which women are contesting with the support of local and international NGOs, it is nevertheless important that generalised statements about the success of popular participation do not go unquestioned.

The 'beautiful dynamic' of popular participation?

The Bolivian LPP was implemented from 1994, and so precedes the Beijing Platform for Action, and the subsequent focus on gender mainstreaming. In this regard, the LPP could be seen as particularly forward-thinking, in that it is a law that was written with an explicit intent to integrate gender awareness and gender equality into the political process.

Lauded as the most important and successful of a series of reforms initiated in the late 1990s, the LPP instituted democratic municipal government on a nationwide basis for the first time (Booth and Piron 2004). In its own words, it sets out to:

> secure improvements in the quality of life of Bolivian women and men, with a more just distribution and better administration of public resources. To strengthen the political and economic instruments necessary in order to perfect representative democracy, facilitating citizens' participation and guaranteeing equality of opportunity in terms of representation of women and men (Secretaría Nacional de Participación Popular 1994, 2).

The LPP created new layers of locally elected municipal government, and devolved 20 per cent of national tax revenue to the local level for participatory community development. It divided the country into over 300 new municipalities, each with its own locally elected leadership, within which local organising committees — known as Territorial Base Organisations (OTBs, also referred to as Area-Based Community Organisations or ABCOs) — were established. The OTBs in each community tend to be pre-existing socio-territorial organisations such as neighbourhood committees (juntas vecinales), and ayllus,[2] or other forms of indigenous territorial organisations officially recognised by the municipal government as representative of a given community or area. These local committees are responsible for producing the annual community development plans (the *Plan Annual Operativo* or PAO) and acting as the interface between local and municipal governance. The municipal government should then use its allotted tax revenue to fund the development initiatives set out in the community's plan.[3]

Although remaining rather vague as to the specific composition of the community committees, all paragraphs in the law indicate that both men and women should be considered eligible and equal participants. Proponents of the LPP argue that these features give the law a progressive thrust in the area of gender relations.[4] It is also believed that, since popular participation is centrally concerned with improving local social services — areas in which women in both urban and rural areas are normally more concerned than men — the implementation of the law has provided a favourable context for the development and increased visibility of women's public roles at the local level.[5]

The real significance of the LPP is that it does provide a genuinely legal basis for women's political participation in local and regional governance. Rather than simply relying on normative entitlements, Bolivian women have explicit legislative entitlement through the LPP to participation in structural decision-making processes.

The impact of the LPP

To some extent, the LPP has provided avenues for the increased participation and visibility of women in decision-making processes at both community and municipal levels. Several positive examples exist of the ways in which women are moving into the spaces created by the law, and beginning to exploit its possibilities.

Under the LPP, municipal plans are expected to include 'women's concerns'.[6] In an attempt to give substance to this provision, the Gender Affairs Sub-Secretariat within the Ministry of Human Development decided in 1995 to target 12

urban and 12 rural municipalities for specific short-term interventions to promote gender awareness in the planning processes. The Sub-Secretariat worked on assessments of gender needs, trained women's rights promoters, and developed Legal Advice Centres in the urban areas. One of the selected municipalities, Entre Rios, in the southern Department of Tarija, is offered here as a good example of what can be achieved when the LPP is applied under favourable conditions. According to the former head of the Gender Affairs Sub-Secretariat, the LPP implementation in Entre Rios has created a 'beautiful dynamic'[7] in which many traditional relationships of ethnic and gender oppression have come to be questioned seriously for the first time (Booth *et al.* 1996). In Entre Rios, the favourable conditions include a strong local Guaraní[8] women's organisation, a powerful indigenous people's organisation, and well-trained facilitators from the Gender and Rural Sub-Secretariats, which work together with local NGOs. The non-governmental Legal Services Network in Entre Rios was used to publicise the opportunities available under the LPP, while also carrying out work on human rights issues.

A second positive example comes from Cochabamba city, the third largest urban centre in the country. Here, there is a markedly greater participation of women in the OTBs than one finds in rural regions. According to municipal government figures, approximately 20 to 30 per cent of the OTB leadership is female, compared with, for example, less than one per cent in rural areas within the Cochabamba Department as a whole.[9] This can largely be accounted for by the presence of both a relatively powerful Women's Civic Committee,[10] and several NGOs working specifically towards the promotion of women's rights within the city itself. These women's organisations have lobbied the municipal government to promote the introduction of 'Gender Secretaries' within the OTBs. Their remit is to raise issues of gendered equality of opportunity at the community level, and encourage women's greater participation in the decision-making processes of the LPP. This is a positive step towards gender mainstreaming, with this role accounting for the majority of the percentage of women in leadership positions in the OTBs.

Overall, these examples indicate that, with the right kinds of intervention, popular participation has the potential to act as a catalyst for positive transformations in gender relations. Having said this, there are still challenges. For example, there is still a long way to go before the Gender Secretaries make a significant impression. I found, for example, that this new leadership role is accorded little real importance within the OTBs themselves — possibly the reason why no men have stood for election to this position — and that the role of Gender Secretary remains vague or unheard of in the minds of the community members.[11] Furthermore, the LPP has not had a positive impact for all women, even in areas in which good work is now being done, and in many areas this work is lacking altogether.

In the following section, I highlight some of the gendered dynamics of the LPP and its implementation at the local level. Then, moving from the particular to the more general, I focus on some of the flaws in the gendered dimensions of the LPP at the point of inception.

Barriers to gender mainstreaming: urban women's experiences

Structural inequalities and constraints arising from differences in women's and men's gender roles and expectations create both practical and strategic barriers to effective gender mainstreaming in development processes. The following examples are based on ethnographic research conducted in urban and peri-urban neighbourhoods on the outskirts of Cochabamba city in 1997. They illustrate the ways in which the drafters of the LPP required greater understanding of the structural barriers preventing women from taking advantage of the opportunities for participation provided by the Law.

Lack of time

The first structural barrier is lack of time. On a practical level, women have less time than men to participate in political processes. Their multiple roles and responsibilities for reproductive and productive work lead to their being differentially time-poor. As a result, women felt they had little or no time to spare to become involved in the LPP, regardless of their commitment to doing so. Women's additional roles as community mangers, including their roles within women's community groups such as the *clubes de madres* or mothers' clubs,[12] tended to be overlooked. These roles were not perceived, by either men or women, as 'political' and so were accorded little social status. As Moser states:

> The fact that men are more likely to be involved in community politics means that the participation of local women as community managers is frequently either invisible or not valued. However, there is also a negative side to women's participation. While their participation is often crucial for project success, this is based on the assumption that women have 'free time' [...] When women fail to participate, it is not women who are the problem [...]. It is a lack of gender-awareness of planners about the different roles of men and women in society and the fact that women have to balance their time allocation in terms of three roles (Moser 1993, 103).

Gendered equality of participation may be written into the text of the LPP, but, unless this participation is practically and strategically facilitated, women's involvement is made particularly difficult. For example, for women to find the time to participate, they first have to perceive themselves, and be perceived by others, as having 'free time' for such purposes. This time is a strategic gender need, in Moser's terms (1993).

In addition, the meetings have to be held at times that fit into women's daily routines: a practical gender need (Moser 1993). The following extracts are from interviews with women who live and work in the resource-poor neighbourhoods of Barrio Colquiri and Ville Sebastián Pagador.

Lourdes[13] is Quechua, originally from a mining family on the Altiplano, but has lived in Barrio Colquiri for over ten years. She is a nurse by training but now spends her time looking after her four children, plus two from her husband's previous marriage. She continues to provide unofficial health care within the community. Her husband is a car mechanic in a small garage near the centre of Cochabamba. Lourdes has been going to the neighbourhood *club de madres* for approximately three years and is now treasurer of the group:

> 'I know about the junta vecinal but I don't participate. I don't have time to go to the meetings. [...] There are more men in the juntas vecinales because women are more inhibited, they inhibit themselves and they don't go to the meetings. They have to cook, wash, so many things to do in the house, whereas men dedicate themselves to their work outside, come home at about 5 or 6 pm and then they can go to the meetings, whereas women stay at home watching the kids. But it seems to me it doesn't have to be like that. We also have to participate. Little by little women will participate more'
> (Barrio Colquiri, March 1997).

Lidia is the President of the *club de madres* in Ville Sebastián Pagador and a juice seller in the neighbourhood market. She does not participate in the *junta vecinal*, and has little knowledge of the LPP. Her daily routine again exemplifies the time-poverty that many women experience. In spite of this, Lidia was the person who initially established and runs the neighbourhood *club de madres*:

> 'I leave the house to sell at 7am until 2pm. Before 7am I prepare the juices to sell. I wash clothes, clean the house, then I come to sell. I wake at 5.30am. At 2pm I wash the clothes, clean the house, then I return here to sell again at 4pm until night. At night I go home to cook dinner or sometimes we eat here in the market. I go to bed at 10pm. I have three sons [...] we are six in all. My husband works as a seller in the centre of town so he doesn't have time to work in the house [...] I haven't participated in the junta vecinal. [The President] doesn't tell us when there are meetings unless it's very important. Those of my neighbourhood, we know almost nothing. We have heard about the Law [LPP] but I don't know very well what it is. They say it is going to be good for us but I didn't find out a lot about it. I haven't heard of the PAO [Plan Annual Operativo]. I haven't participated in anything like that' (Ville Sebastian Pagador, June 1997).

These interview extracts illustrate the ways in which the gender division of labour, and women's and men's different uses and concepts of time, affect women's participation in community politics, and hence the LPP. They also illustrate the ways in which genuine gender mainstreaming necessitates a will to address barriers arising from such differential socio-cultural expectations of gender roles and the lived realities of women's lives.

Ideological barriers to women in politics

What is also clear is that women, despite their time-poverty, are actively involved in 'community' organising — thus termed as opposed to the men's 'political' organising. On an ideological level, the political sphere is perceived as a male domain. Women's community organising is something that both the men and women in the neighbourhoods overlook — or rather, do not apportion significant value to —despite that fact that the work of the women's community groups is frequently both implicitly and explicitly political.

An understanding of the power dynamics and experiences of individuals and groups at both intra- and inter-household levels is crucial if the rhetoric of gender mainstreaming is to be realised. Furthermore, as exemplified by the LPP, planning and policy that is implemented without adequate understanding of such grassroots dynamics can fail to impact positively on key actors in a given target group, and, importantly, fail to understand the reasons for such problems.

Popular participation: missed opportunities for gender mainstreaming?

A critique of many 'women in development' (WID) approaches to development is that they have 'tagged women on' to an existing development process. This lack of a rigorous gender analysis often reinforces or even extends gender inequalities for women. While the LPP was intended to formalise women's political equality of participation through legislative reform — to give them *de jure* political status — it largely ignored the pre-existing structures which deprived women of *de facto* political power in the first place. Consequently, it has failed to address the fact that women are not necessarily in a position to take full advantage of the opportunities for political enfranchisement provided through this law.

The failure to mainstream a gendered perspective throughout the process of planning and implementing the law has had a number of negative repercussions. Most noticeably, what has occurred is that community organisation has become a political arena within which there is, for the first time, a genuine opportunity to control significant resources. There is also an opportunity to recognise and enjoy direct structural relationships with municipal government, and national political parties. In other words, community-level develop-ment and grassroots social organisation is now being accorded much greater impor-tance. It has become an arena in which local leaders can make their mark, potentially able to use this space as a stepping stone towards greater political ambitions. As a result, women now have to compete with men for spaces that were previously relatively ignored because, 'now there is money in these local spaces men are taking more interest and so women are fighting not to get pushed out'.[14]

At these local levels, men always tended to be more visibly in control of decision making, through their acknowledged leaderships of indigenous, union, or neigh-bourhood organisations such as the *ayllus*, *sindicatos campesinos*[15] or *juntas vecinales*. Whilst such organisations were ostensibly responsible for lobbying for infrastructural local development, such as improvements in water supplies or roads, prior to the intro-duction of the LPP their efficacy was limited. This was due to their relative lack of resources, and to the lack of status accorded to these 'feminised' local spaces at the macro political level.

Women, on the other hand, were — and are — frequently the pro-active but largely invisible organisers and facilitators of development and change at a community level. This may be via formal membership of social groups such as *clubes de madres*, in which women work together to, for example, improve family nutrition, provide informal welfare and health care, and create community spaces such as playgrounds and gardens. It may alternatively be through the organisation of informal local networks, developing invisible safety nets amongst resource-poor families in the absence of a welfare state.[16] Since the 1980s there has been a rise of neo-liberal reforms in Bolivia, a subsequent pulling back of the State, and a continued economic crisis. This all means that the work of such socio-functional groups — both the formal and informal networks of predominantly women who engage in this often largely invisible productive, reproductive, and community management work — has become under-recognised. At the same time, as Lind (2002) argues, this work is fundamental to the national social structure. Women's community organisations play a critical part in the socio-economic development of the local arena, but have attracted little acknowledgment of their roles at either the local or national political levels.

The introduction of the LPP provided an ideal opportunity for this (gendered) development work of women at community level to become more formally recognised and resourced. This was not, however, the immediate effect. Instead, what were traditionally defined as female/feminised spaces — as a result of their association with the private/domestic/local spheres — are now, through greater political power and resources, becoming an increasingly contested environment.

As mentioned above, for a community to become part of the popular participation process they first need to register an OTB. One aspect of the Law is that these OTBs should be territorial organisations rather than functional. This raised an immediate gendered bias in terms of who controlled the LPP at the local level. In Bolivia, there tend to exist certain types of community organisation, and these tend to have a marked gendered dimension.

On the one hand, there are neighbourhood committees (*juntas vecinales*), indigenous groups (e.g. *ayllus*), and union groups (e.g. *sindicatos campesinos*). These groups are perceived to be territorial, pertaining to a given area or community, and are seen as the more official representatives of a given community. On the other hand there are organisations formed around a particular social function or interest, into which *clubes de madres* are placed. Whilst almost invariably pertaining to a given area or community, these groups are not formally regarded as territorial. It almost goes without saying that the former are overwhelmingly male-dominated and the latter female-dominated.

Thus, as it was written into the LPP that only territorial groups could be registered as OTBs, this automatically excluded female-dominated community groups. Furthermore, by according new powers and status (via registration as OTBs) to the already male-dominated territorial community organisations, the LPP in some cases led to an increased polarisation of gender roles and powers at these levels. In other words, rather than a valorisation, increased visibility, and enhancement of women's roles at these levels, men were able to appropriate these new, more powerful positions. In doing this they further consigned the 'remnants' of community organising and decision making to women, with a concomitant reduction in their relative status.

In this respect, several criticisms could be raised with regard to the lack of explicit mechanisms written into the LPP, both to guard against the male domination of these political spaces, and to promote equality of opportunity in representation of women and men. Other than the language of gender mainstreaming and recognition of women within the legislation itself, the Law did not provide any special mechanisms or incentives for changing gender relations in a positive direction. It could be argued that, whatever the existing radical potential of the LPP, important opportunities were missed to make it more directly powerful as a strategy to encourage the increased enfranchisement of women into community and municipal leadership roles.

There were three broad thrusts to the argument against more directly and tangibly targeting women in the LPP legislation.[17] First, at the time it was claimed that setting quotas for the participation of women in the OTBs would generate an unhelpful backlash against an already controversially radical reform. A declaration of principle, on the other hand, would provide a basis for a local movement with sufficient support to move ahead in an effective way. However, we have since seen the establishment of the 'Law of Quotas' in 1997, which does specifically set quotas for women as candidates in national political parties (Booth, Clisby, and Widmark 1997). This suggests that, political will allowing, the LPP could also have included certain targets within its own legislation.

A second argument for the lack of specific targets for women's participation being named was that higher rates of illiteracy and lower levels of education among women presented serious obstacles to women's leadership participation that could not be legislated away.[18] Issues of illiteracy and a lack of formal training do pose problems when establishing new forms of governance and leadership, and women are statistically over-represented in illiteracy tables. However, I would suggest that these problems are by no means gender-specific, and do not constitute sufficient cause not to specifically target women as potential community leaders.

Indeed the same standard does not seem to apply to male leaders. In Independencía in the High Andes, for example, a Quechua male counsellor was elected to the new municipal government. He spoke almost no Spanish (the official language of politics, in which all legislation is written), and had very little formal education, literacy, or training in leadership skills.[19] There was no serious suggestion that only well-educated, Spanish-speaking men should be allowed to stand for municipal government. Any such suggestion would have been met with widespread outrage from the majority indigenous, rural communities across the country. Illiterate women are inherently no less capable of leadership than illiterate men, and the way forward is to provide essential capacity building for all candidates, regardless of gender.

A third issue which most directly discriminates against women's participation in the LPP is that of the definition and recognition of the OTBs. As discussed above, the problem for the overwhelming majority of women's organisations throughout Bolivia was that they were not deemed to qualify officially as OTBs, because they were classed as neither territorial nor as representing the whole population of a given *barrio*. It was claimed that this problem stems from an objective reality of gender relations in Bolivia, rather than from any insensitivity to gender issues on the part of the legislative team.[20] This 'objective reality' is that indigenous Andean traditions of domestic consultation are based on the concept of complementary gender roles: the public/private spatial dichotomy. This, it is argued, leads to less purely patriarchal patterns of decision making than appears at first sight (Taipinquiri 1996; Harris 2000).

I find this fundamental premise flawed. However, for the purposes of this critique, even if we accept that the distinction between female-dominated functional groups and male-dominated territorial groups is a technically legitimate argument, it remains problematic. In reality, community-based women's groups, although not officially precluding membership by women from different communities, do tend to be overwhelmingly territorial in as much as they pertain to a given neighbourhood. It would be a relatively simple matter to make these organisations officially territorial and, as such, qualify as OTBs on these grounds. An argument against this was that, whether territorial or sectoral, women's community organisations do not represent both men and women in a given neighbourhood in the same way as *juntas vecinales* officially do. This is despite the fact that *juntas vecinales* tend to be overwhelmingly male-dominated organisations.[21] There is an important and wider issue here: it appears to be more acceptable for all-male or predominantly male committees to purport to represent the whole than it is for female-dominated groups to do so.

The evolution of gender mainstreaming in popular participation

So, to return to the question posed in the title: is the LPP an example of effective gender mainstreaming or not? On the one hand, the three arguments against more directly targeting women (discussed in the previous section) demonstrate the ways in which, despite the rhetoric, the LPP reflects deeper, insidious gender biases operating within society. We have seen how the LPP can actually serve to reinscribe unequal gender relations through a series of biases and assumptions written into the Law. The LPP talked about gender mainstreaming, but did not ensure that this actually occurred by providing adequate capacity building in a comprehensive and sustainable way. It shied away from positive-action measures, failed to incorporate an analysis of women's and men's gender roles, and made assumptions about women's capabilities and their forms of community organising that discriminated against women from the outset. Thus, despite the laudable intentions of the LPP, not enough was done at the crucial stage of implementation to facilitate the equality of participation and decision making that it claimed to advocate.

This is not to say that the LPP has not begun to break down the gendered barriers to women's formal participation; indeed, in some cases, women have managed to exert greater leverage. More broadly, the Law has generated a momentum of enhanced citizenship and participation which 'is acknowledged as something irreversible' (José Barriga, Vice Minister for Popular Participation and Municipal Strengthening, cited in Imparato and Ruster 2003, 326). Despite its flawed beginnings, it does seem that something of a groundswell of action around capacity building, including some work on gender issues, is occurring across the country. As more and more people become aware of their rights under the LPP, increasing numbers of local actors are calling for these rights to be realised. As Verónica Cutipa, a community group leader in Cochabamba, points out, 'while before the Law we knew nothing, we have learned something, at least to complain, to demand the rights that are ours by law' (cited in Imparato and Ruster 2003, 326).

The LPP process has received support from a range of international government and non-government agencies, and in some areas across the country there are now several local and international NGOs working to build upon the gendered dimensions of the Law.[22] One of the NGOs being supported is the Instituto Femenina de Fomento y Formación Integral (IFFI), a regional NGO working in Cochabamba to promote women's rights and provide training for women. It has been running a series of workshops to raise awareness among women of their rights, responsibilities, and opportunities available under the Law. In Ville Sebastián Pagador, for example, IFFI helped a group of women to present their demands for development initiatives to be included in the annual PAO. Their plans included a scheme for the construction of a community and training centre. The male leadership of the OTB said their plans were unrealistic because the zone had much more pressing priorities, such as water and sewerage systems, which would require all the LPP funds for the next few years. Undeterred, the women approached the Mayor directly and explained their plans and the situation. The Mayor eventually agreed to provide 50 per cent of the necessary funding for the project, if they were able to raise the other half. Examples such as this provide evidence of how, in some areas, women are moving into the spaces created by the LPP and beginning to exploit the possibilities of the Law. It is unlikely, for example, that without the LPP providing the institutional framework, the women from Ville Sebastián Pagador would have prepared a proposal which, although it did not make it through the official channels of the LPP, reached the level of municipal planning and became a future possibility.

However, the LPP failed to integrate appropriate capacity-building mechanisms into the legislation in an effective and systematic way. It has thus been left to both local and international NGOs to step into this gap in recent years in ways that provide a patchy and relatively *ad hoc* national picture.

Nevertheless, there are instances where the goal of gender mainstreaming in popular participation in Bolivia is closer to being realised. Although these instances do currently tend to be exceptions to the more general pattern, since women's participation in the political sphere at any level remains relatively limited, they nevertheless demonstrate the possibilities that have been opened up by the Law. What has also been demonstrated across the region is that, once aware of their rights under the LPP, women are keen to become involved in decision making. It is certainly not the case that, as I was told by several male community leaders, 'women simply don't want to participate'.[23]

To mainstream gender concerns properly into popular participation is undoubtedly a long, slow process, which would call for major political and financial investment over many years. However, the experience thus far has generated some interesting dynamics. While the LPP has resulted in some women being pushed out of development processes at local levels, there have also been tangible advances for other women's groups. As Lind (2002, 246) notes, 'some women's NGOs that are subcontracted by the state have [...] benefited to a large degree, in political as well as financial terms. Such is the case of IFFI in Cochabamba.' She goes on, however, to sound a warning note: 'This perceived power is not necessarily permanent, it depends on future political relationships and policies and IFFI may or may not retain this power.'

Lind is right to be cautious: as we have seen at macro-development levels, it is all too easy to provide a gendered discourse at the policy level, but with little concomitant 'engendering' of development processes. It seems clear that the LPP will not provide proponents of gender mainstreaming with a textbook example of success. However, there is significant energy and commitment among both women and men across Bolivia to use the Law as a tool to strengthen local-level decision making, and within this, to promote greater opportunities for gender equality in participatory planning.

Notes

1 The distinction between practical and strategic gender interests or needs has become an important reference point in 'gender and development' (GAD) discourses. See particularly Molyneux (1985) and Moser (1993).

2 *Ayllus* are ancient forms of indigenous territorial organisation in the Andean region. *Ayllus* tend to be associated with the Aymara, one of the largest indigenous groups in the region and dominant on the Altiplano (Ticona *et al.* 1995; Taipinquiri 1996; Vasquez 1998). Bolivia is unique among its South American neighbours in that approximately 60 per cent of its population is indigenous, with the largest groups being Quechua (30 per cent) and Aymara (25 per cent) (UNICEF 1994; Freedomhouse 2004).

3 For a fuller explanation of the LPP, see Booth *et al.* 1996; Booth *et al.* 1997; Kohl 2003.

4 Taken from interviews with the Gender Affairs Secretariat between 1994 and 1997, and with Ivonne Farah, former Vice-Minister for Gender Affairs and Sonia Montaño, formerly Sub-Secretariat of Gender Affairs, Ministry of Human Development, La Paz, 1996.

5 Taken from interviews with the Secretaría Nacional de Participatión Popular and the Sub-Secretaría de Asuntos de Genero, La Paz, 1995–7.

6 Law No. 1551, Law of Popular Participation, Article 14, 20 April, 1994.

7 Taken from an interview with Sonia Montaño, La Paz, formerly Sub-Secretariat of Gender Affairs, Ministry of Human Development, La Paz, 1996.

8 The Guaraní are the third largest indigenous group in Bolivia, with a population of approximately 5,000

people concentrated in the eastern lowland Department of Chuquisaca. However their territorial boundaries spread across Paraguay, Brazil, and Argentina and their total population is estimated at approximately 80,000 (Survival 2005). They have a distinct language and culture, and Guaraní was given official language status in Paraguay in 1992 in recognition of the fact that it has been the dominant lingua franca there for centuries (Wearne 1996).

9 Taken from interviews with Osvaldo Montaño, Director de Gestion Territorial, Municipal Government of Cochabamba, May 1997.

10 The Women's Civic Committee is a sub-committee of the municipal Civic Committee and is largely made up of prominent women in the city. The Committee is dominated by women of Mestizo and Spanish descent, with a higher socio-economic status than indigenous urban women. Those involved tend to be educated, professional women who are also often related to men within municipal politics. The Women's Civic Committee, while technically non-governmental, is perceived as being linked to local government and sees its role as that of lobbying for both women's issues and wider social concerns to be addressed within municipal government.

11 Taken from ethnographic research conducted in Cochabamba during 1996 and 1997.

12 *Clubes de madres*, or mothers' clubs, have a long history in Bolivia. They primarily serve as a grassroots social and welfare-based support network for women and their families across the nation. *Clubes de madres* can also have a political edge and engage in political protest, lobbying for socio-economic and political change. See, for example, Lind 2002.

13 Individual names have been changed.

14 Carmen Zabalaga, Co-ordinator of the Instituto Femenina de Fomento y Formación Integral (IFFI), March 1997, Cochabamba, Bolivia.

15 *Sindicatos campesinos*, or peasant unions, are largely male-dominated groups with significant power, particularly in rural areas.

16 Bolivia is one of the poorest countries in Latin America, with 63 per cent of Bolivians living below the poverty line, and 42 per cent (3.3 million) living in conditions of extreme poverty. The average annual income of poor people stands at $290, with 70 per cent of the population living on less than $2 a day (Republic of Bolivia 2001). Bolivia is an aid-dependent country in which, according to Nickson (2002, cited in Booth and Piron 2004), the scale of financial and institutional aid dependency is comparable to that of an average African 'heavily indebted poor' country. In 2000, net assistance to the country stood at 5.8 per cent of GNP (Booth and Piron 2004) and the budget deficit rose to 8.6 per cent in 2002, well above IMF limits (Byron and Zolezzi 2003). Wealth is concentrated in the hands of five per cent of the population, and levels of both poverty and unemployment have worsened in the past decade (*ibid.*).

17 Taken from interviews conducted with a range of Bolivian commentators, academics, and legislators between 1994 and 1997. See also Booth *et al.* 1996; Booth *et al.* 1997.

18 Taken from interviews with the LPP legislators, the Secretaría Nacional de Participatión Popular.

19 Taken from research conducted in Independencía in 1996.

20 Ruben Ardaya Salinas, Director de Fortalecimiento Municipal, Secretaría Nacional de Participación Popular, La Paz, 1996.

21 According to the president of the National Confederation of Neighbourhood Associations (CONALJUVE), Juan José Diez de Medina, there is a mandatory 50 per cent female quota in its appointments. This has not, however, been translated into *de facto* participation in decision-making roles, and neighbourhood committees remain predominantly male-dominated.

22 Danish, Dutch, Swedish, Swiss, Canadian, and US agencies are supporting the LPP. The Canadian International Development Agency (CIDA), for example, approved 14 projects across the country between 1999 and 2003, worth $725,000, through its Gender Equity Fund (GEF). The GEF strategy is to encourage the incorporation of policies and resources for gender equity, and in June 2000 CIDA established a gender equity programme in Cochabamba with six participating local NGOs.

23 Drawing on ethnographic research (1995–7), I found this tended to be the prevailing view of a range of male community leaders in across the country.

References

Booth, D., S. Clisby, and C. Widmark (1996) *Empowering the Poor Through Institutional Reform? An Initial Appraisal of the Bolivian Experience*, Stockholm: SIDA/Stockholm University

Booth, D., S. Clisby and C. Widmark (1997) *Popular Participation: Democratising the State in Rural Bolivia*, SIDA/Stockholm University, Stockholm

Booth, D. with L-H. Piron (2004) *Politics and the PRSP Approach: Bolivia Case Study*, Working Paper 238, London: Overseas Development Institute

Byron, G. and G. Zolezzi (2003) 'South American Regional Gender Fund, Phase II Evaluation Country Study: Bolivia', La Paz: Canadian International Development Agency

Freedomhouse (2004) 'Freedom in the World: Bolivia', www.freedomhouse.org (last checked by author March 2005)

Harris, O. (2000) *To Make the Earth Bear Fruit: Ethnographic Essays on Fertility, Work and Gender in Highland Bolivia*, London: Institute of Latin American Studies

Imparato, I. and J. Ruster (2003) *Slum Upgrading and Participation: Lessons from Latin America*, Washington: World Bank

Kohl, B. (2003) 'Democratizing decentralization in Bolivia: the Law of Popular Participation', *Journal of Planning Education and Research* 23: 153-64

Lind, A. (2002) 'Making feminist sense of neoliberalism: the institutionalization of women's struggles for survival in Ecuador and Bolivia', *Journal of Developing Societies*, 18(2-3): 228-58

Neimanis, A. (2003) *Gender Mainstreaming in Practice: A Handbook*, Regional Gender Programme of the United Nations Development Programme's Regional Bureau for Europe and the CIS (UNDPRBEC), UNDP

Molyneux, M. (1985) 'Mobilization without emancipation? Women's interests, state and revolution in Nicaragua', *Feminist Studies*, 11(2), pp227–53

Moser, C. (1993) *Gender Planning and Development: Theory, Practice and Training*, London: Routledge

Republic of Bolivia (2001) 'Bolivia Poverty Reduction Strategy Paper', La Paz: Government of Bolivia

Secretaría Nacional de Participación Popular (1994) Ley de Participación Popular: Reglamento de las Organizaciones Territoriales de Base, La Paz: Ministerio de Desarrollo Sostenible y Medio Ambiente, Articulo 1:2

Survival (2005) 'Guaraní', www.survival-international.org/guaraní, (last checked by author, May 2005)

Taipinquiri (1996) *Cosmovisión Andina: Expresión y sentimiento espiritual andino-amazónico,* La Paz: Centro de Cultura, Arquitectura y Art

Ticona, E., G. Rojas, X. Albó (1995) *Votos y Wiphalas: campesinos y pueblos originarios en democracia*, Laz Paz: Fundación Milenio/CIPCA

UNICEF (1994) *Children and Women in Bolivia*, La Paz: UNICEF

United Nations (2001) 'Supporting Gender Mainstreaming: The Work of the Special Advisor on Gender Issues and Advancement of Women', United Nations, www.un.org/womanwatch (last checked by author March, 2005)

Vasquez, G. R. (1998) 'The Ayllu' in Apffel-Marglin/PRATEC (eds.) *The Spirit of Regeneration: Andean Culture Confronting Western Notions of Development*, London: Zed Books

Wearne, P. (1996) *Return of the Indian: Conquest and Revival in the Americas*, London: Cassell

Freedom for women:
mainstreaming gender in the South African liberation struggle and beyond

Shamim Meer

The liberation struggle in South Africa highlighted racial and class oppression as key causes of poverty, inequality, and a lack of rights for most South Africans. Drawing on the language of the struggle, women political and trade union activists brought attention to their oppression and exploitation as women, and were able to place non-sexism alongside non-racism and democracy as key liberation principles. However, while men in these organisations ostensibly accepted the idea of non-sexism, they were not ready to change their behaviour or give up their power, and women activists met with ongoing resistance. During the negotiations for democracy, women drew on their experience of the years of struggle and were able to ensure a high proportion of women in parliament, influence the country's constitution, and advocate the establishment of State machinery to mainstream gender equality. However, in the post-apartheid era of reconstruction and development, both the demobilisation of protest movements and the emphasis on the technical aspects of development stand in the way of gender mainstreaming via the State.

Introduction

It is important for us to unite women committed to a non-racial, non-sexist, democratic South Africa. Otherwise we will find ourselves in the same situation as women from other countries in the post-liberation era. After having struggled together with their men for liberation, women comrades found their position had not changed. We need to assert our position as women more strongly now than ever before and we can only do that effectively as one, unified, loud voice.
(Feroza Adam in Meer 1998, 124)[1]

A cornerstone of the national liberation struggle in South Africa during the years of apartheid was mass mobilisation and mass action. Entire communities took part in work stay-aways, workers engaged in strike action, students boycotted classes and closed down academic institutions. Women engaged in all of these struggles as workers, students, and community members, and, as they did so, they pursued an additional struggle — the struggle for women's liberation from oppressive gender relations.

Through their active involvement in the liberation movements and their careful strategising, women activists were able to shape the mainstream of political ideas. By the mid-1980s, despite dominant Marxist and nationalist views that women's rights would divert and weaken the struggle (Wieringa 1995; De Mel 2001; Hutchful 1999), non-sexism was made an aim of the mainstream struggle — at least at the level of language. However, although they won the support of some men in their efforts to mainstream women's rights within the liberation movements, women found that the gains they made were constantly under threat. Their strategies were shaped not only by their experience of apartheid capitalism, but also by the resistance of men in the liberation organisations.

Building on their activism during the years of struggle, women political activists played a key role in the negotiation process that marked the transition from apartheid to a democratic South Africa. Women campaigned for their inclusion in the negotiations.

Through their participation, they ensured that gender equality was enshrined in the new South African constitution, and that machinery to mainstream gender equality was in place.

However, progress on gender equality made during the transition has not automatically been transformed into unambiguous gains for women within the post-apartheid era of development. Women's organisations were demobilised, and were no longer a force to be counted on in efforts to mainstream gender equality. The shift from struggle to development has resulted in technical approaches to what are essentially always political problems: the rights of workers, poor people, and women. It seems that, taken out of the arena of struggle into the State and bureaucracy, gender equality has become a technical concern.

A history of women's organising in the context of struggles against apartheid

Women have a long and successful history of organising in South Africa. Their struggles ensured that gender equality became a central concern in the years leading up to the development of the post-apartheid South African State.

In the 1960s, the severe repression of the apartheid State led to the outlawing of resistance organisations such as the African National Congress (ANC). But by the early 1970s trade unions, student and community-based organisations had mushroomed across South Africa. In the 1980s local struggles in individual factories and isolated communities came together, and national trade unions, student, civic, and women's movements were formed. These were able to grow despite State repression, including states of emergency, bans, detentions, and assassinations of political activists.

In addition to being active in organi-sations as workers, students, and community activists, women organised in separate community groups, in women's forums in trade unions, and in women's wings of liberation movements. While struggles for liberation attacked the lack of civil and political rights, women were successful in inserting their demand for equality as women within these mainstream struggles.

Women organise in trade unions

The mainstream liberation movements, led by men, had an interest in women's involvement because they needed to boost the numbers involved in the struggle to end the national and class oppression of black people and workers. In the case of trade unions, their bargaining power with management hinged on their ability to sign up 51 per cent of the workers in a work place as paid-up union members. Where women constituted a sizeable proportion of the workforce, the union could only attain majority when women became union members. It was thus important for the unions to recruit and sustain the membership of women workers.

In establishing the right of women to join trade unions and political organisations alongside men, the principle of women's equality was established. This allowed women to talk of equal rights in other spheres of their lives. As greater numbers of women entered the trade unions and community-based resistance organisations, they began to raise concerns that could not be ascribed completely to the racist apartheid State, or to capital. They spoke of the problems they faced in their work places connected with equal wages, maternity leave, and childcare. They spoke of the difficulties they experienced in being activists. These included restrictions placed on women's movement and time by boyfriends and husbands, their heavy workloads arising from household responsi-bilities and paid employment, and the attitudes of fellow workers, trade union officials, and leaders who saw them as inferiors — as 'tea makers instead of speech makers'. They spoke of problems of sexual harassment and rape in their homes, in their workplaces, and in their communities.

In 1983 women brought the 'private' concerns from their homes and communities to the public attention of a national education conference of the Federation of South African Trade Unions (FOSATU) for the first time. A speaker at this Conference, MamLydia Kompe, spoke of the problems she encountered as trade union organiser. Her fellow trade unionists saw her as inferior, expected her to make their tea simply because she was a woman, and were resistant to women in leadership positions. In addition women faced obstacles in their homes; the biggest obstacle in her own life was a husband who did not want her to attend union meetings. She spoke out against these practices, noting that:

> 'A woman is a human being... we appeal for equal rights... We don't want to be inferior' (Meer 1998, 69).

A second speaker, Tembi Nabe, highlighted the unfair division of domestic labour which consumed women's time. A woman had to get up early to make tea for her husband, prepare water for washing, make the bed, wash the baby, take the baby to the child minder, prepare herself for work, get to work and be harassed all day, perhaps as a domestic worker. Then at the end of the day she picked up the baby, cooked, cleaned, washed, ironed. Even though her husband was home, Tembi Nabe reported that:

> 'he doesn't even think of fetching the baby. He makes it a point that every time he comes back from work his little darling is next to him — that is his bottle of whiskey or brandy' (ibid.).

In challenging deeply held ideas of women's roles and place in the home and political activism, a vision of a different gender order was emerging, suggesting new ways of being women and men. The notion of exploitation was extended into analyses of relationships within the home

and the community. Many men at this meeting found it difficult to accept that working in one's own home for husbands and children could be exploitation. As one man said:

> 'it is tradition among our people. It is unacceptable to most of our people that a man should look after children and do the washing.' (ibid.)

Other men, however, supported the women trade unionists, as the following comments show.

> 'We don't have to use tradition. If a man is home early he has all the rights to make the fire and cook for the children.'

> '[I]f we both go out to work, but when we get home it is my time to rest and my wife's time to carry on working, I don't think the struggle will go on.' (ibid.)

One of the conference organisers, Grace Monumadi, emphasised that women should not be scared and should act now to break down divisions between women and men workers, because:

> 'we don't want to wake up in years to come to find that women have been left out of the struggle.' (ibid.)

Women continued the discussion begun at this conference over the following years, within their unions and the Federation. They set up women's forums to support each other, and to strategise ways of ensuring that women's equality would be taken up by the trade union movement. In their workplaces, women agitated for — and won — maternity benefits, thus advancing their reproductive rights.

Women brought their concerns to national gatherings of women,[2] and to the National Congresses of the Federation. They changed the nature of the discussion in trade union congresses, making political struggles of 'personal issues' such as contraception, abortion, childcare, maternity, sexual harassment, and domestic violence. They made calls that men should share childcare and housework, as the domestic burden on women did not allow them to participate in the economy and society. They also called for fair wage employment policies and women's representation at all levels of the economy and society. They asserted that there should be equal relationships between women and men in the Congress of South African Trade Unions (COSATU)[3] and in the country as a whole. They campaigned for women in leadership, and they raised the matter of sexual harassment and rape of women within the trade unions.

Women organise in communities

Women in community and political organisations were able to change the nature of the discussions in these organisations also. In addition to taking up struggles around rent, water, and childcare, women campaigned against rape and violence against women.

In 1986, the Port Alfred Women's Organisation organised a stay-away from work to protest at poor handling of a rape case by the police: the rapist had not been charged. The women emphasised how important it is to talk about rape and sexual assault openly. They noted that sexual assault is 'another kind of oppression' (*ibid.*, 81). In 1990, when gang rapes were on the increase, Soweto church women marched in protest carrying placards which read 'sexual abuse is a crime against humanity' (*ibid.*, 86).

At regional level, organisations such as the Natal Organisation of Women (in then Natal), the United Women's Congress (in the Western Cape), and the Federation of Transvaal Women (in the then Transvaal), were formed in the early 1980s. They worked for the removal of all laws and customs that act against women. These organisations came together in 1987, in the United Democratic Front[4] (UDF) Women's Congress. Their participation in the male-led UDF educated members about women's oppression, and enabled women's concerns to be raised in all UDF meetings and organisations.

They aimed to increase women's skills and confidence, and do away with all forms of discrimination based on sex.

In 1990, the ANC women's section (who were in political exile, the ANC having been banned in the 1960s), women from UDF-linked organisations in South Africa, and the Women's Committee of the Dutch Anti-Apartheid movement organised the Malibongwe Conference in Amsterdam. The conference aimed to make sure that women's freedom was part of the struggle for national liberation. It called for housework and childcare to be shared by men and women, reasoning that only then would women be able to take part fully in political activism. There was agreement that freedom for women would not be an automatic outcome of national liberation, that cultural and traditional practices that oppress women must be fought, and that in addition to laws to protect women's rights there was a need to change attitudes. The conference made a call that sexism be fought as seriously as racism.

Union men resist

While the majority of men in the liberation organisations accepted the notion of gender equality along with worker rights and the rights of black people, they did not expect women to challenge male sexual behaviour, or their prerogative to lead. Calls for women's representation in leadership were resisted by COSATU men, despite continual demands from women, and it was only in 1993 that COSATU had its first woman in national leadership. To this day, COSATU has resisted calls for quotas for women in leadership.

Resistance to confronting exploitative sexual behaviour of men in the unions was made clear when an affiliate, the Transport and General Workers' Union (TGWU), brought a resolution on a sexual code of conduct to the COSATU 1989 Congress. In introducing the resolution, the male TGWU president spoke out against what some men saw as their unquestionable right. He called attention to a growing problem of the sexual exploitation of young women union members by senior male trade union leaders. The young women entered these as serious relationships, but were soon abandoned by the men, and this resulted in women members leaving the union. The resolution sparked four hours of heated debate in the male-dominated Congress, and was the only resolution not passed at the Congress. Some men felt that the resolution should never have been brought to Congress. A minority believed that women's oppression was a reality, and, like racism, needed to be tackled head on. The compromise reached was that the committee drafting a general code of conduct for COSATU members would look into the issue. The resistance of COSATU men to addressing sexual exploitation in their ranks was further highlighted by the fact that it took seven years after this Congress for COSATU to adopt a policy against sexual harassment.

In the face of such resistance, women trade union members continued to organise themselves in separate women's forums in the unions affiliated to COSATU. However, these attempts to build their skills and confidence were constantly under threat. In 1988, plans to set up a national women's structure within COSATU were subverted by male leadership on the grounds that this would undermine community-based women's organisations.

At the 1990 Congress of the National Union of Metal Workers of South Africa (NUMSA, a COSATU affiliate), male delegates argued strongly that women's structures should close down because they were not performing well. Women delegates pointed out that the education committees (of which the women's structures were a part) were not performing well, yet there was no suggestion that education structures close down.

At the 1991 COSATU Congress, two union affiliates recommended that COSATU

women's structures disband in the interests of integrating women's concerns. Women resisted, arguing the necessity for organising separately as women. After much discussion the Congress decided to set up gender forums, made up of women and men members, to function alongside the existing women's forums (Lacom *et al.* 1992). Confusion over the different roles of gender and women's structures had the effect of weakening women's organising efforts, and diverted attention from the issues that women had thus far managed to bring into the mainstream of trade union forums.

The language of gender had entered the world of the trade unions in the late 1980s. As COSATU women noted, without the recognition of power imbalances, it shifted the focus from the fact that men benefit from the oppression of women, and that women are disadvantaged; it can blunt women's struggle and disguise the fact that men must give up privileges; and it can result in men taking control of women's struggles, for example as the dominant actors and ideologues in gender structures (*ibid.*). COSATU women continued to argue the need for women to lead the struggle for an end to women's oppression and exploitation, noting that to leave the struggle for gender equality to men is like leaving the struggle against apartheid to whites:

'The motor for driving action on gender has to be women' (ibid., 50).

ANC men resist

Like COSATU women, ANC women found resistance from men in the ANC to their calls for increasing the numbers of women in ANC leadership. In 1990, there were no women among the six national office bearers of the ANC, and women made up only 18 per cent of the National Executive Committee (NEC). The ANC Women's League (ANCWL) raised this as a problem at the 1990 ANC Consultative Conference, and got the male leadership to agree in principle that affirmative-action measures needed to be considered. The ANCWL canvassed male leaders to support the proposal they planned to bring to table at the 1991 ANC Conference. The proposal was that at least 30 per cent of the positions on the NEC of the ANC be filled by women. Although senior ANC male leaders agreed to support the proposal, they did not actually do so. At the 1991 conference, ANC women found themselves isolated, and their proposal rejected. In the heated debate that followed the introduction of their proposal on quotas, delegates argued that women were not ready to lead, that there were few women of leadership quality, and that women must prove themselves. Angry, disappointed, and let down, ANC women told the conference that similar arguments had been used by the apartheid regime to keep power in white hands.

As a result of their defeat at the 1991 Conference, the ANCWL recognised the need to organise at grassroots level on an ongoing basis, so as to make sure that there was greater support for women's equality. They also saw the need to build a broader coalition of women to influence the negotiations already under way for a democratic South Africa. Their defeat brought home the reality that unequal social relations within society enter even liberation movements such as the ANC. Raymond Suttner, head of ANC political education, noted in 1993 that there was a lot of abuse of women in the democratic movement. Women were beaten and raped, and while lip-service was paid to gender equality, people in the ANC were still at the 'beginning stages' of understanding the full significance of this. In particular, there was not an adequate understanding of what this would mean in their personal lives (Meer, 1998).

Negotiations and a constitution for a new South Africa

The shift from apartheid to a democratic political order took place through a negotiated settlement which began with talks between the apartheid government, the ANC, and other key liberation movements. These talks started soon after the ANC was unbanned. Between 1991 and 1994, the talks moved into more structured negotiations, and culminated in an election date being set for April 1994.

As the key organisations moved to the negotiating table, new political formations were established in the country. The ban on the ANC having been lifted, returned exiles and released political prisoners joined UDF activists in establishing the ANC within the country. UDF organisations, including the UDF women's organisations, were encouraged to disband, so that their members could build ANC and ANCWL branches.

In the course of the creation of this new political landscape, community-based women's organisations that had been key in the preceding years were demobilised. COSATU unions entered an alliance with the ANC, and contributed to the negotiations as an alliance partner, resulting in the loss of an independent voice on the part of trade union women.

At its launch in 1991, the ANCWL prioritised action to contribute to the country's constitution. However, realising that they stood only a slim chance of influencing the negotiations and the drafting of the country's constitution on their own, ANCWL leaders initiated the formation of the Women's National Coalition (WNC). This brought together some 60 organisations (including women's wings of political parties, church women, and organisations such as the Young Women's Christian Association). The WNC played a significant role in influencing the constitution, and shaping the machinery intended to mainstream a commitment to gender equality in the new State.

By drawing on gains made by women in preceding years in placing non-sexism on the liberation agenda, the WNC was able to ensure that women's equality took precedence over customary law in the country's constitution. It campaigned for, and won, national machinery to advance gender equality, including an Office on the Status of Women, a Commission on Gender Equality (CGE), and gender focal points in all government departments. It also played a key role in sensitising political parties on the importance of women's votes, and the advisability of increasing the numbers of women on their electoral lists. The ANC agreed on a one-third female quota on their list of parliamentary candidates. In the first democratic election, in 1994, an ANC victory resulted in 101 of the 400 seats in the national assembly going to women — making South Africa count among the countries with the highest proportion of women in parliament.

In 1994, the WNC launched the Women's Charter. By this time, most of the key leaders of the WNC had become members of parliament, or had joined the ranks of other tiers of government; their energies were dispersed in national politics and away from feminist interests. Without effective leadership, and a unifying issue to sustain the coalition, hopes that the charter would be the focal point for sustaining a strong and effective women's movement were not realised (Meintjes 1996).

While the gains made by the WNC are clearly significant, it is important to note its limitations in taking up the calls made by women in the UDF and COSATU over the 1980s and 1990s. The WNC was a new organisational formation representing a broad coalition, within which neither the former UDF women's organisations (which had by now collapsed into the ANCWL), nor COSATU women, participated. The influential voices represented in the coalition tended to be those of a middle-class, more conservative constituency, which had never engaged in the liberation struggles. Calls by COSATU, UDF, and ANC women on reproductive rights and shared housework were not key issues for the WNC, and it was not able to arrive at consensus on abortion. Added to this, the WNC was engaging in a new terrain that required technical and legal expertise around negotiations and constitution making, within the broader negotiations framework, which emphasised a middle ground rather than battles between opposing forces. Former activists within the WNC made shifts to learn new skills, or were marginalised as technical expertise took over.

Post-apartheid South Africa

As a result of women's active involvement in the struggle for liberation and the strategic intervention of organised women during the negotiations, the post-apartheid government policy espouses a strong commitment to gender equality. There is a high proportion of women in public office. However, in the context of reconstruction and development it has been difficult to sustain the organisation of women, and this has weakened women's ability to ensure the goal of gender equality, despite their gains.

The first democratic parliament in 1994 had one of the largest proportions of women parliamentarians; the constitution of the country guarantees equal rights between women and men; and there exists an impressive array of mechanisms to promote women's advancement. These include:

• the parliamentary committee on the Improvement on the Quality of Life and the Status of Women, established in 1996 to oversee the implementation of the Convention on the Elimination of All Forms of Discrimination Against Women and the Beijing Platform for Action;

- the Commission on Gender Equality (CGE), established in 1997 to monitor and review legislation and the gender policies of publicly funded bodies to ensure that women's equality is promoted;

- the Office on the Status of Women (OSW), established in 1998 to co-ordinate and provide guidance to gender units within national government departments and provinces, and to initiate policy-oriented research;

- gender focal points in most line function departments;

- almost all line function departments have made some attempt to include women's concerns in their white papers;[5] some have produced gender policies, and many have conducted some form of gender training for staff.

It has taken time to set up these institutions, and an overarching constraint is that they lack resources. The CGE and OSW are poorly resourced. Gender units and focal points lack senior management support, and lack clarity on gender goals. Gender equality is often read as a numbers game, with a focus on making sure that the composition of State institutions reflects the race and gender demographics of the country (Meer 2003).

Further, these structures are often not staffed by feminist or political activists who would be more willing to address the goal of gender equality as a political project requiring the transformation of existing relations between women and men. Seidman (2003) notes how, within the CGE, women wanting to construct a feminist project within the State came up against those concerned with a project of national development. This resulted in an approach which avoided direct challenges to gender inequality, and instead emphasised service to women within the framework of existing gender relations.

Given their great hopes that equality for women would be created through the State, women leaders from the trade unions, community-based organisations, the UDF, ANCWL, and WNC entered national or provincial parliaments. Women entering the State were, however, overwhelmed by the demands of these institutions and spent more time learning the rules of the game than challenging them. The language of State institutions encourages the technical, and does not easily admit the political. Concerns about sharing housework and childcare with men, and challenging men in order to transform gender relations, are not a part of the technical approach dominant in State-influenced structures. As Baden and Goetz (1997) note for other contexts, the preoccupation is with procedures rather than the power relations that result in women's subordination. Gender became professionalised, and gender experts became de-linked from grassroots constituencies and not accountable to them.

Women's organisations of the years of struggle are no longer vocal or visible, and thus do not serve as either pressure or resource to State-created institutions. Outside government and parliament, South African women have been most notably active in campaigns to combat violence against women and promote reproductive rights. They have contributed to the development of legislation and policy to address violence against women and termination of pregnancy. However, in areas such as economic policy and land reform, where advancing women's rights threatens male privilege far more directly, women have not constituted an organised force, nor have they made gains.

In the new era of reconstruction and development, power relations have been de-emphasised and development is increasingly defined in technical and legal terms. The struggle was seen as over, once South Africans had won political rights. In my view, growth and market efficiency, and not political struggle, are now advanced by the ANC government as solutions to poverty and inequality. As Miller and Razavi (1998) note for other contexts, gender mainstreaming which suggests win–win scenarios has gained ground over more confrontational ideas, which are rooted in structural understandings of women's and workers' oppression and exploitation.

That the technical arenas of policy and law are not sufficient to address gender power relations, and that struggles need to continue both inside and outside the State, is illustrated in Michael Blake's (2001) observations that South Africa is a deeply patriarchal masculinist society with pervasive ideas of male superiority and privilege. This is evidenced in survey results showing that 40 per cent of South African Municipal Workers' Union (a COSATU affiliate) members admitted abusing their partners in the past ten years. Blake notes that the world of the union is one of sexist jokes, unwanted sexual advances, male domination at meetings, male abuse of power, male devaluation of women's contributions, the ignoring of women's concerns, and sidelining of women. Men in COSATU saw quotas for women as a direct threat to male domination. The approach to gender equality is to get men to assist in women's development, but not to address their own oppressive masculinity.

Conclusion

Through their organisation and strategic actions, South African women were able to make non-sexism a key goal and value of the national liberation struggle. They ensured that gender equality was enshrined in the constitution, and that an array of gender machinery was put in place to mainstream gender in the new State.

However, as Alvarez (1989) notes in relation to Brazil, it has been difficult to translate the fervour of the political struggle to the new context of post-apartheid development. In a context where development is seen as apolitical, where the emphasis is placed on technical solutions, and where the State is seen as the vehicle for the promotion of gender equality, there has been little space left for women's activism outside of state arenas.

Yet development and the attainment of gender equality are both political matters. To advance these goals there is a need for struggle both at the level of ideas and practice. To take up such struggles, there is a need for strong women's organisations which have as their focus the transformation of gender power relations.

Shamim Meer worked as a political and human rights activist during the years of apartheid, in communities and with trade unions in South Africa. Since 1994, she has worked with NGOs and some government departments in addressing women's rights within programmes such as land reform, trade and industry, and rural development. She continues to search for ways of linking notions of struggle to questions of development.

Notes

1 These are the words of Feroza Adam — a feminist activist, who was to become a member of parliament in South Africa's first democratic parliament in 1994 — to a national conference of trade union and community-based women in March 1990.

2 A National Women's Congress in 1988 and a National Women's Seminar in 1989.

3 COSATU was established in 1985, bringing together FOSATU affiliates and other independent trade unions, such as the National Union of Mineworkers and the South African Allied Workers' Union.

4 An umbrella body of organisational affiliates resisting apartheid.

5 White papers are produced by government line function departments and spell out their broad policy frameworks and priorities.

References

Alvarez, S. (1989) *Engendering Democracy in Brazil: Women's Movements in Transition Politics*, New Jersey: Princeton University Press

Baden, S. and A.M. Goetz (1997) 'Who needs sex when you can have gender? Conflicting discourses on Gender at Beijing', *Feminist Review* 56: 3-25

Blake, M. (2001) 'The Mal(e)aise in COSATU' in 'GETNET Network News', February, Cape Town: GETNET

De Mel, N. (2001) *Women and the Nation's Narrative: Gender and Nationalism in Twentieth Century Sri Lanka*, Colombo: Social Scientists Association

Hutchful, E. (1999) 'Marxist responses to the challenge of gender relations' in A. Imam, A. Mama, and F. Sow (eds.) *Engendering African Social Sciences*, Dacca: Codesria

Lacom, SPEAK, and COSATU (1992) *No Turning Back: Fighting for Gender Equality in Trade Unions*, Johannesburg: Lacom, SPEAK, COSATU

Meer, S. (1998) *Women SPEAK: Reflections on our Struggles 1982-1997*, Cape Town, Kwela Books

Meer, S. (2000) 'Which Workers, Which Women, What Interests? Race Class and Gender in Post Apartheid South Africa', paper presented at Project CES/MacArthur Symposium on Reinventing Social Emancipation, Coimbra, Portugal, 23–26 November 2000

Meer, S. (2003) 'Putting EU and UK Gender Policy into Practice – South Africa paper for Closing the Gap', London: One World Action

Meintjes, S. (1996) 'The women's struggle for equality during South Africa's transition to democracy', *Transformation* 30: 47-63

Miller, C and S. Razavi (1998) 'Introduction' in C. Miller and S. Razavi (eds.) *Missionaries and Mandarins: Feminist Engagement with Development Institutions*, London: ITDG

Seidman, G.W. (2003) 'Institutional dilemmas: representation versus mobilisation in the South African Gender Commission', *Feminist Studies* 29: 3

Wieringa, S. (1995) *Subversive Women: Women's Movements in Africa, Asia, Latin America and the Caribbean*, New Delhi: Raj Press

Gender mainstreaming in government offices in Thailand, Cambodia, and Laos: perspectives from below

Kyoko Kusakabe

In this article, I aim to examine the ways in which gender concerns have been 'mainstreamed' into government activities. I focus on three countries in the Greater Mekong Sub-region: Thailand, Laos, and Cambodia. While gender mainstreaming policies are in place at the national level in these countries, the 'evaporation' (Longwe 1995) of such policies at the lower levels has been a problem. The article concentrates on challenges of implementation which exist at provincial/commune and department levels. Drawing on the experience of middle- and low-level government officers, I argue here that policy evaporation occurs partly because of lack of political commitment to gender mainstreaming at different levels. Another problem is that the concept of gender mainstreaming itself remains vague, and is thus difficult to translate into action.

In 1997, the Economic and Social Council of the UN defined gender mainstreaming as, first, the *process* of assessing the implications of any planned action for both women and men. Second, it is a *strategy* for making women's concerns and experiences an integral dimension of the design, implementation, monitoring, and evaluation of policies and programmes in all political, economic, and social spheres, ensuring that women benefit equally with men.[1]

In the last few decades, various approaches to gender mainstreaming have been developed and implemented in different countries and organisational settings. These have included appointing gender focal points among staff; conducting training in gender sensitivity and gender analytical skills; developing gender policies and methods of gender-responsive planning; and carrying out gender-sensitive monitoring and evaluation, through identifying gender indicators, collecting gender-disaggregated data, and, recently, gender budget analysis.

Many problems regarding gender mainstreaming have already been identified by practitioners and scholars alike (for example, Rai 2003; Goetz 2001; Miller and Razavi, 1998). Problems include the weak influencing power commanded by gender focal points, lack of resources, the evaporation of gender policies when it comes to implementation, and the difficulty of gender mainstreaming in the face of gender-biased organisational culture and discourse. Some scholars have even questioned whether gender mainstreaming is co-opting the feminist agenda, instrumentalising and diluting it, and thus doing more harm than good for gender equality (Standing 2004; Miller and Razavi, 1998).

In this article, I briefly survey the efforts made to address gender issues in government offices, in Laos, Cambodia, and Thailand. These cases may not be representative of the overall effort that is taking place in these countries. However, it is hoped that they will serve as food for thought. In particular, they highlight the need to give more attention to the importance of the activities of middle and lower field-level government officers.

Cambodia

Cambodia was under socialist rule from 1979 to 1993. Under the socialist system, Cambodia had a Women's Association of Cambodia (WAC) — a mass organisation of the socialist government, which extended from central to village level. It was involved not only in political campaigning, but also in relief work, especially supporting poor widows, and destitute women.

In 1993, when Cambodia abandoned socialism for democracy, a Secretariat of State for Women's Affairs was established immediately after the first general election. The Secretariat was later upgraded to a Ministry of Women's Affairs in 1996.[2] Many former WAC staff members were absorbed into the structure of the Provincial Department of Women's Affairs, which operated in the provinces under the Ministry of Women's Affairs. In 1999, the Ministry produced a five-year strategic plan, *Neary Rattanak*.[3] In this, it defined a policy advisory role for itself on gender issues in relation to all line ministries, local government, and public institutions. The direct social-service delivery function inherited from WAC was abandoned. Due to a lack of national funds, almost the entire budget for implementation of activities of the Ministry of Women's Affairs comes from international project support.

There are four major types of gender mainstreaming activities that have been carried out by the Provincial Department of Women's Affairs (PDWA), with technical support from the Ministry. These are: gender training; working with gender focal points in government ministries; giving input into planning in ministries; and information sharing and awareness raising about women-specific issues, including violence against women.

Gender training has been conducted at all levels from the Provincial Department staff to villagers. In general, I found that people expressed discomfort about training their peers, even within the Ministry, preferring to train people whom they perceived as lower in status than they were. The Ministry trained trainers who are now based in the Provincial Department, with the aim that they would, in turn, train district, commune, and village-level people. However, the training occurs only when and where there are funds available from donors. Often, gender training is the sole gender activity undertaken at community level.

There is no doubt that gender training is important, but activities and achievements beyond training were not often found.[4] The heavy focus on gender training was due to lack of clarity on the part of provincial and commune-level gender staff about their mandate to promote gender equality. Gender training is a concrete activity, in which they have experience, and are confident that they can do well. As a result, their activity report amounts to a list of training sessions, which they state had an underlying aim of covering all government staff and villages in the province.[5]

Gender focal points have been appointed in each Provincial Department of the other government ministries, and at the village commune level. In the ministries, gender focal points are mostly lower-level officers, and normally do not have any departmental budget allocated. The focal points were not chosen for their expertise on gender issues, but have undergone gender training. They have regular meetings with staff from the PDWA, but I found that the meetings did not always provide them with clear guidance about what they should be doing in their departments. At commune level, there is lack of knowledge of the existence of gender focal points. None of the women we interviewed in the villages even knew that there was a gender focal point in the commune council.

Frustration due to the lack of clarity in roles is felt within the commune, as well as by provincial level officers. One gender focal point in the commune council replied to our question on what she does as a gender focal point[6] as follows: *'I don't do anything, because there is no budget. I am not instructed from above what I should do. They (PDWA) sometimes give me posters for domestic violence and trafficking. I went to the villages to distribute these. Now it is finished. I have been to PDWA meeting several times. But it has now been a long time since I have last met them… No, no one in the villages comes to me to discuss about their problems…'*

Lack of concrete work beyond gender training, and lack of clarity on the mandate of gender focal points, means that staff acting as gender focal points are often not assessed positively on their performance by colleagues. One male officer at commune level said: *'Yes, we have a gender focal point. But I do not know what she is doing. She does not come to office regularly. She is busy'.* Such statements that they do not know what the gender officer is doing, and their perception that gender officers are busy or sick, implies that male officers view gender officers as not productive, and not contributing to the activities of the council.

Participation of the PDWA in the planning process of government departments was achieved at two levels. Within government ministries, staff participated directly in meetings or supported gender focal points to give input. At local level, planning is carried out by commune councils, and includes a series of discussions with villagers.[7] Final decisions on development activities that are to be implemented are made at the district integration workshop. Here commune councils discuss their plan with provincial/district departments, as well as other organisations working in the area. The PDWA fed into this local planning in various ways, including supporting the gender focal points in the commune council to raise gender issues, and (with the Ministry for Women's Affairs)

developing a gender mainstreaming checklist to be used during the planning process. The checklist reminds planners to consider whether women will be able to participate in, and benefit from, proposed activities.[8]

There are significant challenges involved in undertaking these activities. In order for the PDWA to provide necessary inputs to other departments' plans, it needs extensive knowledge of other sectors' work, in addition to knowledge and experience of planning. If the gender focal points are to carry out the work, they need knowledge of the gender issues relating to their particular sphere of work. Often, their level of knowledge makes it impossible to do anything beyond noting and reporting on the number of women participants in commune activities. However, it would not be fair to conclude that the difficulties that PDWA and commune gender focal points have in raising gender issues in planning processes arise merely from their lack of knowledge. It is unrealistic to expect the provincial and commune-level gender focal points to have a profound ability in policy analysis and planning, especially with the absence of any technical and political support. Lack of financial resources for gender focal points discourages attempts to take more innovative or proactive actions, and also contributes to their low status in the province and commune. But without opportunities to discuss their ideas and without support for translating their ideas into action, it is difficult to come up with activities beyond training, even if there is a budget.

The final activity of PDWA is to disseminate information on gender issues, and run awareness-raising activities in communities, on issues such as domestic violence. Despite the policy of no direct implementation of projects in communities, field-level activities are carried out by PDWA on women-specific problems such as domestic violence, trafficking of women and children, and vocational training and skill improvement for women. These activities are often carried out with enthusiasm, and there is increased awareness of issues like domestic violence and trafficking of women and children.[9] However, these activities are often implemented separately by PDWA and gender focal points at commune level, and do not necessarily lead to or influence the way they work with other departments and other commune council members.

Overall, the Cambodia case suggests that the gender mainstreaming process is understood in vague terms. As a result of successful gender training, awareness and willingness to work on gender issues is high among provincial/commune-level government officers. However, concrete activities that should take place are unclear, and thus people who want to work on gender issues are discouraged and lose momentum.

Lao People's Democratic Republic

Lao PDR has a Women's Union: a mass organisation under the socialist government. In the beginning, its focus was to promote traditional gender norms, and it concentrated on national security (Saphakdy 2005). It was given a wider mandate in 1991, when its role in promoting the equal rights and advancement of women, and responding to women's needs, was recognised under the Constitution. In 1993, at its Third National Congress, Lao Women's Union adopted a commitment to gender awareness and equity.

As one of the two institutions in Lao PDR[10] formally recognised as having responsibility for advocating women's rights and gender concerns, the Women's Union has a unique opportunity to influence the policies, plans, and practices of both government and non-government organisations. One of the strengths of the Women's Union is that it has a strong network from the national to the village level. Although membership to the Union is automatic after

a Lao woman reaches 17 years old, the active members are the elected representatives of villages. Some Women's Union village representatives are active, and work diligently as volunteers. However, since most of the work of the Women's Union is unpaid and time-consuming, some representatives feel over-burdened.[11]

In most development projects in Lao PDR, Women's Union provincial and district staff are put in charge of women's concerns or gender issues. For example, in an integrated rural development project in Northern Lao PDR,[12] a Women's Union officer, seconded to the project, was in charge of both micro-credit and gender issues. This particular project was successful in supporting women's weaving activities, which led to a large increase in household cash income. The Women's Union, with its vast network in the village level, could expand the scale of project activities much faster than any other component of the project. However, later on, the price of woven cloth dropped, and the activity became less lucrative. At the same time, export tax was introduced, further adversely affecting the weaving industry. Although the weaving activity was successful at the beginning, in the absence of co-ordinated support by the State for the activity, the women weavers were left at the mercy of the market. The support for weaving was confined to the Women's Union, and was not integrated into other sectors such as finance, commerce, and agriculture. As a result, timely support for export of woven cloth or alternative employment for women was lacking.

Another example of an activity of the Women's Union comes from the Governance and Public Administration Reform (GPAR) project in Luang Prabang. The GPAR project began in 2002. It aims to improve governance through enhancement of human-resources management, financial management, office environment, planning and co-ordination, and service delivery capacity. Project documents specify that the project will work closely with the Gender Resource Information Development Centre of the Women's Union, and will take gender issues into consideration. The need to increase the number of women in responsible positions, and to give training and development opportunities for women, was specified in the documents. However, when translated into action, the only activity that was carried out under gender main-streaming was two gender training sessions (Saphakdy 2005).[13]

The emphasis on awareness raising indicates the project's underlying assumption that if officers are informed of gender concepts, they will be more sympathetic and co-operative towards gender initiatives and will also take up gender-responsive activities. However, Saphakdy's study (2005) shows that there is no relation between a positive attitude towards gender equality initiatives and the number of times individuals have attended gender training.[14] It should be noted that the training provided for them was focused on awareness raising and did not provide them with concrete ideas on what to do in the field or in the workplace.

The Lao case shows that having a nationwide women's network does not necessarily carry the message of gender equality throughout society. It also does not make it easier for gender issues to be incorporated into the work of various sectors and departments. Moreover, the legacy of mobilising women for national goals, without challenging traditional gender norms, has been hard to remove from the organisational culture of the Women's Union. The former focus of the Union was to support nation building. Such efforts to bring women to contribute to certain causes can be easily shifted towards a focus on women contributing to the well-being of the family/community or to national economic development. However, it is more difficult to shift to the ideology of protecting women's rights and the political process of changes in gender relations. The change in direction of the Women's Union discussed above is not necessarily understood or agreed by all its members. Therefore, the Women's Union network itself does not necessarily lead to the initiation of a political process for gender mainstreaming.

Thailand

In Thailand, the first official national mechanism for advancement of women — the Office of the National Commission on Women's Affairs (ONCWA) — was set up in 1989 under the Prime Minister's Office. In 2002, ONCWA was transferred to the Ministry of Social Development and Human Security. It was combined with the Family Development Office, and the new body was named the Office of Women's Affairs and Family Development (Tamthai 2005).

As part of its effort to mainstream gender concerns in all ministries and departments, Chief Gender Equality Officers (CGEOs) have been appointed in all government agencies, at both ministry and department levels. CGEOs are to oversee gender integration in policy and planning processes in their respective government departments (Bhongsvej and Putananusorn 2003).

In the case of the Department of Fisheries (DoF), the Director of the Personnel Division was appointed as CGEO. His work started with collecting gender-disaggregated data on the staff working in the Department. During a workshop with DoF officers, it was repeatedly emphasised that integrating gender perspectives is the policy of the Department, even though there is no written policy to this effect yet. The Department is active in the Mekong River Commission (MRC) Fisheries Programme, which itself has a gender policy and strategy. This promotes gender-disaggregated data collection, and supports the Regional Network for Promotion of Gender in

Fisheries (RNPGF) (Sriputinibondh *et al.* 2004). Until quite recently, the CGEO did not have any link with the RNPGF.

In the Inland Fisheries Research and Development Bureau of DoF, there are two people who are directly involved in the RNPGF. Within DoF, these national network co-ordinators have not been given the human and financial resources to work on gender mainstreaming. They have attended regional trainings and workshops, conducted several research activities, presented research on gender issues in national fisheries conferences, and held workshops with DoF staff who are interested in gender issues. Yet currently, the designated research areas in the Department focus on areas such as aquaculture and fisheries management, but do not cover areas of research on social issues. This means that even if DoF researchers examine social issues related to fisheries and aquaculture, this is not recognised as an achievement relevant to assessing individual staff members for performance or promotion. As a result, there is no great incentive to carry out research on gender-related topics in DoF.

There is clearly a mismatch between knowledge, skills, connections, motivation, and position inside DoF for gender main-streaming. Additionally, there is a general understanding that even though taking gender concerns into consideration is a policy of the Department, it is not a main priority. All this makes it difficult for those who are motivated to mainstream gender to bring about further achievements and changes. Better co-ordination to overcome the mismatch, empowerment of lower-level officers to voice their needs and ideas for change, and recognition and rewarding of initiatives, could all improve the motivation of staff. Lobbying for the opportunity to do social science related research needs to be done internally through the co-ordination and co-operation of people with different skills, knowledge, and positions.[15] If social issues relating to fisheries and aquaculture were on the agenda, this would allow officers to integrate gender concerns into their daily work.

Conclusion

Below, I summarise some of the many learning points which emerge from the three case studies.

The importance of national policies to local-level implementation

In the three countries studied, at the national level there are gender main-streaming structures in place, including gender focal points, national machinery for the advancement of women, gender units, and gender policy. This article, however, focused on gender mainstreaming processes at the department and provincial/commune level — which has attracted relatively less attention in the gender mainstreaming debate — to trace what has happened at this level. The importance of establishing national-level policies on gender equality is well recognised in bureaucracies. The logic is that if policy, practices, procedures, and incentive structures change at national level, it will be relatively easy to effect similar changes at the lower levels of government. Yet the cases show that the existence of national-level policies and strategies for main-streaming do not necessarily ensure implementation at the departmental and provincial/commune level. I have argued that one of the barriers to mainstreaming a concern for gender equality in the government bureaucracies studied is that the realities of middle- and lower-level government officers are often neglected. The lower-level officers are the ones who are directly in contact with village women and men, but what they should be doing is often not stipulated. Less effort is focused towards them and their daily work than towards national-level work on developing gender policy, reforming organisational structure, and running gender training sessions.

New institutional structures for gender mainstreaming: the pros and the cons

In Lao PDR, the Lao Women's Union is seen as the organisation responsible for gender mainstreaming. Even though Lao does not have a large NGO population, the Women's Union is able to reach out and mobilise a large number of women, since it is a mass organisation with a long history (established in 1955). However, this long history in itself presents challenges for the Union's transformation into an organisation with a mandate to promote gender equality in all spheres of life. This transition is difficult. Given the sector-based planning practices of government in Lao PDR, and its new mandate, the Women's Union needs to work with other departments to ensure that gender issues are mainstreamed into their work. But because the Women's Union is a well-established institution, with independent work that it has been doing for decades, and because other sectors also do not see the need to change the way they work, it is difficult to adjust to performing this new role. It is even more difficult for the lower-level Union officers. They still feel they lack clarity regarding their gender main-streaming roles, and the relationships that they should be forging with colleagues in other government departments.

In contrast, Cambodia created a new institution for gender mainstreaming. But the process of transition from socialism spelled the end of the women's association set up under the socialist system. This led to the loss of the nationwide network of women which had been a feature of the association. The case study emphasised that the new institution has to depend on other government departments to influence its agenda and facilitate contact with its constituency of grassroots women. These departments have extension officers in the field, for reaching out at the village level, while PDWA does not. Most gender main-streaming discourse remains at the philosophical level, and is not being translated into concrete action at the field level. Not being able to work and show concrete achievements gives a negative impression to their colleagues in the commune. This, together with the budgetary constraints discussed earlier, leaves field-level gender officers with low self-esteem and status.

Challenges concerning the donor-driven nature of gender mainstreaming

In Cambodia and Lao PDR, gender mainstreaming is often donor-driven. The sustainability of the initiative as the consequence of donor dependence is one problem. Another problem is that the opportunities provided by these donor-driven initiatives are not translated into routine procedures in government offices. Especially among the lower-level govern-ment officers, there are problems in identifying what should be done in practical terms. Often, people are left trying to work this out on their own.

Gender training as the sole or main activity in gender mainstreaming

The case studies provided evidence of a very heavy emphasis on gender training in mainstreaming. In Cambodia and Lao PDR, with the support of donor agencies, gender training at the lower levels has been conducted, and gender is no longer a novel concept. Gender awareness has therefore been achieved to some extent. Although gender training may be necessary, it is not sufficient to ensure that gender concerns are mainstreamed into government bodies and their activities. Administering gender training can, indeed, even be seen as a strategy which enables those staff charged with gender mainstreaming to avoid addressing the reality of resistance to the idea that government should work to promote gender equality. Initially at least, training presents an easy way out in these situations: the deadlock can be blamed on a lack of understanding and support from other members of the organisation and wider society, which can be 'solved' by training.[16]

It is important that other concrete activities for gender mainstreaming (especially routine activities) are introduced in the middle and lower levels of government. Ongoing small activities related to gender mainstreaming at the field level create a favourable environment to allow initiatives to grow. For example, regular home visits in communities/groups by technical staff, (such as district agriculture extension officers) can begin a process of transformation. Through discussion and consultations with poor village women, practical gender concerns and their links to unequal gender power relations emerge. Each visit can develop this dialogue. Such routine discussions by technical staff need to be accompanied by regular meetings with officers trained in, and in charge of, gender mainstreaming. Such initiatives already exist, or are planned, in many areas in each of the three countries. However, all will need formal recognition and reward. Routine, concrete actions in the field lead to better gender analysis, better planning, and improved clarity in the concept and meaning of gender mainstreaming.

Challenges in monitoring women's participation

Beyond gender training, the only other activity commonly undertaken in the three countries is to promote women's participation in village and community meetings. All three countries have a large-scale involvement of women in productive activities — in fisheries, in agriculture, and in manufacturing work — but this is often on discriminating terms.[17] In addition, in all three countries women often participate in meetings already, either because they are required to,[18] or because women are at home more and thus more available than men for meetings. Hence, promoting women's participation in productive and community work in the villages does not in itself challenge existing gender power relations as much as might be expected. While monitoring the quality of women's participation and taking steps to improve it might be a good strategy, in general the focus on participation remains quantitative. It is limited to documenting the number of female and male participants in different events. Better knowledge of the national and local contexts in countries on the part of all involved in gender mainstreaming, including international donors, is critical.

Kyoko Kusakabe is Associate Professor, Gender and Development Studies, School of Environment, Resources and Development, Asian Institute of Technology, P.O.Box 4, Klong Luang, Pathunthani 12120, Thailand.
Email: kyokok@ait.ac.th

Acknowledgement

The author would like to thank Ubolratana Suntornratana, Veena N., Toshiko Hamano, Girija Shrestha, and Theonakhet Saphakdy for their comments and inputs on the early draft of this article. Veena N. is also acknowledged for her help in English editing. The author is also grateful to the editors for their useful comments and inputs.

Notes

1 Report of the Economic and Social Council for 1997, A/52/3, 18 September 1997, chapter 4 'Coordination Segment: Coordination of the policies and activities of the specialized agencies and other bodies of the United Nations system'. See www.un.org/documents/ga/docs/52 /plenary/a52-3.htm

2 It was renamed the Ministry of Women's and Veterans' Affairs in 1998, but in 2004 reverted to Ministry of Women's Affairs.

3 This may be translated from Khmer as 'women are precious gems'.

4 It is noted, however, that with the few resources allocated to gender activity, training is one of the limited options available.

5 Interview in Northwest Cambodia, December 2004.

6 Interview in Takeo Province, April 2004.

7 Cambodian administrative levels are village, commune, district, and province.

8 Interview with commune gender focal point in Northwest Cambodia, December 2004; and in Central Cambodia, April 2004.

9 Village leaders say that after the domestic violence training, domestic violence cases in the village decreased. However, this is often based on perceptions. Although many people know about the problem, the effect of training and campaigns on the actual, and not reported, number of domestic violence and trafficking cases is still not clear.

10 Lao National Commission for Advancement of Women is the other institution that has an official mandate for the advancement of women.

11 Unlike the village chief's work, the work assigned to Women's Union representatives is unpaid, tedious work, such as collecting contributions from each household for village ceremonies. Even though it does provide status in the village — since being a representative reflects other women's assessment that one has a good personality and economic standing — the workload can be so heavy that some representatives are not able to continue for long.

12 Study conducted in March 2000 and January 2001.

13 These two training sessions are those that were targeted at the staff members of the project. A gender component was developed in the village management training programme, and provided to senior officials in the village level.

14 Although there was little difference in attitudes among officers who received or did not receive gender training, Saphakdy reported village women expressing that their men are now more helpful at home. Saphakdy also noted that since there were only two gender trainings conducted during the project period, significant change in attitude might not be a realistic expectation. Gender training assessment in Cambodia (Kusakabe and Chim 1999) showed that there is a direct relation between the number of gender trainings organised and positive attitudes towards integrating gender issues in work. However, the number of gender trainings attended was related to the attendee's position: those who were working as gender officers or focal points received more training. Therefore, it is difficult to conclude whether it was the effect of the training or their positions which made them work more positively on gender issues.

15 The author would like to express her gratitude to Ms. Ubolratana Suntornratana for her input.

16 It is recognised also that gender training provides an incentive for officers to work positively on gender equality. In countries where government salaries are low, the per diem and travel allowance paid to them for participation in training is considered significant.

17 For example, men's wages are 23 per cent more than women's on average in Cambodia (Godfrey et al. 2001, 11). According to the 1998 salary survey by the National Statistics Office in Thailand, in enterprises of 1,000 persons and over, women were earning 59 per cent of men's income level, while for enterprise of 100–299 persons, the figure was 65.5 per cent.

18 In Lao villages, some make it a rule that any household that does not attend village meetings will be fined.

References

Bhongsvej, M. and S. Patananusorn (2003) 'Strategies for gender mainstreaming: the case of Thailand' in *Putting Gender Mainstreaming into Practice*, Bangkok: Economic and Social Commission for Asia and the Pacific

Godfrey, M., S. So, S. Tep, D. Pon, C. Katz, S. Acharya, C. D. Sisowath, and T. Hing (2001) *A Study of the Cambodian Labour Market: Reference to Poverty Reduction, Growth and Adjustment to Crisis*, Working paper 18, Phnom Penh: Cambodia Development Resource Institute

Goetz, A. M. (2001) *Women Development Workers: Implementing Credit Programmes in Bangladesh*, New Delhi: Sage Publications

Kusakabe, K. and C. Chim (1999) 'Evaluation Report on CARERE/SEILA Gender Sector Training, Cambodia', CARERE/UNDP, June

Longwe, S. H. (1995) 'The evaporation of policies for women's advancement' in N. Heyzer (ed.) *A Commitment to the World's Women: Perspectives on Development for Beijing and Beyond*, New York: United Nations Development Fund for Women

Miller, C. and S. Razavi (1998) 'Introduction' in C. Miller and S. Razavi (eds.) *Missionaries and Mandarins: Feminist Engagement with Development Institutions*, London: Intermediate Technology Publications in association with the United Nations Research Institute for Social Development

Rai, S. (2003) 'Institutional mechanisms for the advancement of women: mainstreaming gender, democratizing the state?' in S. M. Rai (ed.) *Mainstreaming Gender, Democratizing the State?: Institutional Mechanisms for the Advancement of Women*, Manchester: Manchester University Press

Saphakdy, T. (2005) 'Mainstreaming Gender into Governance and Public Administration Organizations: A Case Study of Governance and Public Administration Reform Luang Prabang Provincial Pilot Project, Lao PDR', Master's thesis, Asian Institute of Technology, Thailand

Sriputinibondh, N., K. Kaing, Nguyen Thi Bich, K. Deeburee, N. Liepvisay, W.D. Hartmann (2004) 'Gender Mainstreaming in the MRC Fisheries Programme', paper presented at the 7th Asian Fisheries Forum, 30 November–3 December 2004, Penang, Malaysia

Standing, H. (2004) 'Gender, myth and fable: the perils of mainstreaming in sector bureaucracies', in 'Repositioning Feminisms in Development', *IDS Bulletin* 35(4): 82-8, Brighton: Institute of Development Studies

Subrahmanian, R. (2004) 'Making sense of gender in shifting institutional contexts: Some reflections on gender mainstreaming', in 'Repositioning Feminisms in Development', *IDS Bulletin* 35(4): 89-94 Brighton: Institute of Development Studies

Tamthai, P. (2005) 'The Role of National Mechanisms in Promoting Gender Equality and the Empowerment of Women: Thailand Experience', proceedings of United Nations Division for the Advancement of Women (DAW), 'The Role of National Mechanisms in Promoting Gender Equality and the Empowerment of Women: Achievements, Gaps and Challenges', 29 November–2 December 2004, Rome, Italy

Woodford-Berger, P. (2004) 'Gender mainstreaming: What is it (about) and should we continue doing it?', in 'Repositioning Feminisms in Development', *IDS Bulletin* 35(4): 65-72, Brighton: Institute of Development Studies

Is there life after gender mainstreaming?

Aruna Rao and David Kelleher

In the world of feminist activism, the time is ripe for reflection and review. We need to ask why change is not happening, what works, and what is next. This article points to the fact that while women have made many gains in the last decade, policies that successfully promote women's empowerment and gender equality are not institutionalised in the day-to-day routines of State, nor in international development agencies. We argue for changes which re-delineate who does what, what counts, who gets what, and who decides. We also argue for changes in the institutions that mediate resources, and women's access, voice, and influence. We outline key challenges, as well as ways to envision change and strengthen the capacity of State and development organisations to deliver better on women's rights.

In the last decade, efforts to make the development 'mainstream' work for women have resulted in impressive gains as well as staggering failures. In the wake of Beijing Plus Ten,[1] numerous reviews document the strategic partnerships forged between the women's movement and policy reformers in the process of putting equity and women's rights at the heart of development debates (UNRISD 2005; Millennium Project Gender Task Force on Education and Gender Equality 2005). Women have made striking gains in getting elected to local and national governance bodies, and entering public institutions; girls' access to primary education has improved sharply; and women are entering the labour force in increasing numbers.

Under the banner of gender mainstreaming in institutional practice, there are numerous examples of positive outcomes for women's lives, beyond policy measures.

They include bringing women to the discussion table during the Burundi peace process; strengthening or establishing organisations and networks to promote gender equality in mainstream agencies; mainstreaming gender issues into law reform processes in Botswana (including national policy regarding HIV/AIDS); gaining greater visibility for women's work through the census in Nepal, India, and Pakistan; and protecting widows and orphans from dispossession on the death of the male 'owner', by supporting primary-justice mediation processes in Malawi. In Rwanda, where women were systematically raped and murdered during the civil war, women have gained 49 per cent of the seats in parliament and formed local women's councils elected solely by women.

The problem is that these examples are not the norm. Practices that successfully promote women's empowerment and gender equality are not institutionalised into the day-to-day routines of State and international development agencies.

More important are the myriad, insidious ways in which the mainstream resists women's perspectives and women's rights. Economic orthodoxy promoting unmanaged, export-led growth through competitive market capitalism, free trade, and fiscal austerity — including the drastic reduction of government social spending — has hurt poor women most (Elson 2005). Governance reforms have not forced States to address their accountability failures when it comes to women's access to resources and services. For the most part, institutional reform still means fiscal and administrative reforms rather than making systems work better for the poor, including women.

In South Africa, where Gender at Work[2] has organised numerous consultations over the past three years, the unease generated by the gap between promise and reality is palpable. Feminist activists speak of the fundamental difficulty in shifting the paradigm of patriarchy within which they operate, and the resultant high fall-out and burn-out. They tell us that they have only managed to chip away at how power is exercised — there is no major shift here. They point to the enormous contradictions they see between good gender equity policies and high numbers of women in positions of power, and some of the highest levels of violence against women in the world. In India (where Gender at Work is also active) social justice activists point to the rise in the power of the State and right-wing politics, and an accompanying decrease in commitment to human rights principles.

At the level of formal institutions, whether they are trade unions, NGOs, women's organisations, community-based organisations, State bureaucracies, or corporate structures, not much has changed either. Organisational structures tend to reinforce the power of a few, who, for the most part, are unwilling to give up the privileges of power. Even when power is shared, decision making remains in the hands of a small number of senior people who, in our experience, are less and less interested in gender equality. Moreover, management discourse dominates institutional life. The strength of traditional management theory, and organisational development thinking and practice, is to focus on efficiency and results. Its weakness, particularly as applied to social-change organisations in many Southern contexts, is that it does not explicitly deal with power dynamics or cultural change. Such theory, therefore, cannot help organisations to develop strategic objectives derived from a nuanced analysis of relational and material hierarchies, or bring about outcomes that change those inequalities.

In the world of feminist activism, it is time to take stock and ask why change is not happening, what works, and what does not work. This rethink is happening at a time of unprecedented militarisation globally which has demoted and marginalised work on women's rights. At the same time we are seeing an equally unprecedented mobilisation of citizens against war, and against the negative effects of globalisation, as well as *for* social justice. Campaigns such as the Global Call for Action Against Poverty (GCAP), led by citizen action groups, are focusing attention on accountability of global institutions, and new terms of trade and development. But by and large, these global movements and their grounding notions of citizenship and accountability are gender-blind.

Moreover, while 'citizens' are mobilising, the infrastructure and resources for supporting women's activism to challenge gender power relations in the home, communities, organisations, markets, and the State are being dismantled. The architecture of organisational structure, process, policy, and funding to support women's empowerment and gender equality is being eroded also at international and national levels. At the same time, new aid modalities such as budgetary supports and Sector Wide

Approaches (SWAPs) may make it more possible to cheat on gender equality goals. Gender concerns are falling through the cracks. Institutional change, capacity building, political partnerships, and women's organising are being marginalised in what is, increasingly, a bean-counting approach to development deliverables.

Gender mainstreaming — wedged between a rock and hard place?

Gender mainstreaming is grounded in feminist theoretical frameworks, and its appeal to 'femocrats' and to gender activists was its promise of transformation. But gender mainstreaming has been caught between a rock and a hard place. At a macro level, it is operating in a policy environment which is increasingly hostile towards justice and equity, and which is further feminising poverty. At a meso level of organisations, gender mainstreaming has become a random collection of diverse strategies and activities, all ostensibly concerned with moving forward a gender equality agenda, but often not working in ways we would have hoped. At this level there is still active resistance to the value of women's rights and gender equality goals. Furthermore, where allies exist, their hands are tied by policy priorities, poor infrastructure, and decreased funding levels. Finally, at a micro level, first-generation development objectives are enshrined in the Millennium Development Goals (MDGs). While the MDGs do incorporate measurable indicators for women's empowerment, there are a number of difficulties. First, they narrow the agenda dangerously (by not including violence against women, for example); second, m any governments have not mainstreamed gender equality into the MDGs (other than the one focused on gender equality); finally, focusing on MDGs has pre-empted support for women's organisations and women's organising — the vanguard of the political fight.

The need for political strategising at multiple levels, and deeper, institutional change, highlights the inadequacy of previous strategies. But it is unclear what the new solutions are. Most feminist activists and analysts acknowledge the need for new approaches that address the discrimination brought about by macro-economic policies in employment, wages, and food security. New approaches must also support welfare services that structure opportunities for women, that hold systems accountable, and that allow for learning on the part of women and men. Those approaches are being formulated. They range from calls for a new social contract (Sen 2004), to the creation of innovatively managed market approaches (Elson 2005); and from calls for the transformation of institutions and organisations (Goetz and Hassim 2003; Rao and Kelleher 2002; Millennium Project Gender Task Force on Education and Gender Equality 2005), to a re-energised and re-politicised women's movement. All approaches to bringing about gender equality must have a political component. This is because gender relations exist within a force field of power relations, and power is used to maintain existing privilege. In the remainder of this article we will elaborate on the dimensions of institutional change.

What are we trying to change?

Our understanding of how to work towards gender equality is that we need to change inequitable social systems and institutions. Generally, people now speak of 'institutional change' as the requirement for addressing the root causes of gender inequality. This means changing the rules of the game. These are the stated and unstated rules that determine who gets what, who does what, and who decides (Goetz 1997; North 1990; Rao and Kelleher 2002). These rules can be formal, such as constitutions, laws, policies, and school curricula; or informal, such as cultural arrangements and norms regarding who is responsible for household chores, who goes to the market, who decides on the education of children, or who is expected to speak at a village council meeting. It also means changing organisations which, in their programmes, policies, structures, and ways of working, discriminate against women or other marginalised groups.

Different organisations have focused on one or other of the four areas listed below. Some organisations, for example, work on legal and policy change, while others focus on changing material conditions. In order to bring about gender equality, change must occur both at the personal level and at the social level. It must occur in formal and informal relations. This gives us the following four clusters which impact on each other:

- women's and men's individual consciousness (knowledge, skills, political consciousness, commitment);

- women's objective condition (rights and resources, access to health services and safety, opportunities for a voice);

- informal norms, such as inequitable ideologies, and cultural and religious practices;

- formal institutions, such as laws and policies.

Figure 1: What are we trying to change?

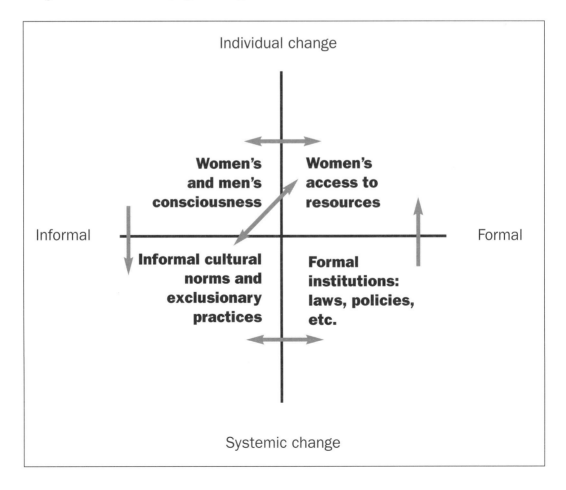

Often we assume that change at one level will lead to change at the others. For example, women who have started and maintained micro businesses often report being more self-confident. However, we also know, for example, that it is possible to have material resources but no influence; and that it is possible to be 'economically empowered' but not free from violence. Sustainable change requires *institutional* change, which involves the clusters of informal norms and formal institutions at the bottom of the diagram. But how does institutional change happen? And most importantly, what is the role of development organisations in that change process? The organisations that support those interventions also exist in the same force field of power. This means that they will require capacities not only to *want* to intervene in a significant way, but also to be *able* to intervene. Typically, it will require an ongoing change process to build and maintain these capacities.

Figure 1 may be helpful in the following ways. First, in an abbreviated way, it shows the whole universe of changes that might be contemplated to enhance gender equality. This can serve as an outline to document how these clusters appear in a particular context. Second, it allows change agents to make strategic choices as to where and how to intervene. Finally, it points to the fact that changes in resources, capacity, and knowledge are necessary, but not sufficient, for sustainable change. Ultimately, changes of formal and particularly informal institutions are required.[3]

What are some of the key challenges of institutional change?

As we reflect on lessons from experience, and contemplate where we go from here, we see four key challenges.

Challenges of institutional change on the ground

Programme and project evaluations point to the difficulty of moving from individual change and learning to social change. They describe the problem of socio-cultural acceptance of ideas of gender equality, the lack of capacity of implementing partners, and the difficulties of attitudinal and behavioural changes at the individual and institutional levels.

Challenges of clarity

A number of analysts have recently pointed out how a lack of clarity endangers implementation of gender mainstreaming strategies (Hannan 2003; Subrahmanian 2004). However, the most pernicious misunderstanding is the separation of gender mainstreaming from women's empowerment work. In the name of mainstreaming resources are being withdrawn from projects focused on women's empowerment. Although much work needs to be done with both men and women, we cannot reduce commitment to programming that focuses on women, because that is where crucial progress towards gender equality is being made.

Challenges of organisational change

The lack of senior-management support; lack of accountability; lack of knowledge and skills among senior staff on gender issues; marginalised, under-qualified, and under-resourced theme groups and specialists are all problems present in organisations mandated to mainstream gender concerns in development.

Challenges of measurement

At one level, there are ongoing difficulties in obtaining sex-disaggregated data. At another level, there is a lack of tracking mechanisms for the relative contributions that a particular project might make to different goals. For example, in a sanitation project, how much of the project budget can be said to be responding to the needs of women? Answering this would require a social-impact analysis at the design stage of the project, and a sophisticated tracking mechanism. At a deeper level, however, is the problem of measuring the intangibles that are at the root of social change of any sort. This is the change in consciousness of women and men, the change in community norms, or the change in attitudes. Incremental changes must be perceived and understood as valued results, knowing that gender equality is a long-term goal.

Beyond mainstreaming to institutional transformation

If there is to be life after mainstreaming, our experience teaches us that it will require transformation at the institutional level. We must come to ideas like empowerment, citizenship, and rights with new eyes and a more overtly political analysis.

Transformation of gender relations requires access to, and control over, material and symbolic resources. It also requires changes in deep-seated values and relationships that are held in place by power and privilege. Transformation is, fundamentally, a political and personal process. Sen (1999) says that institutions limit or enhance poor people's right to freedom, freedom of choice, and action. Without a critical understanding of how institutions need to change to allow different social groups to secure their entitlements and access opportunities for socio-economic mobility, development goals cannot be achieved. From the perspective of poor people, institutions are in crisis and a strategy of change must: '(i) start with the poor people's realities; (ii) invest in organisational capacity of the poor; (iii) change social norms; and (iv) support development entrepreneurs' (Narayan 1999, 223).

Feminist thinking about empowerment directly engages with resources, power, ideology, and institutions (Batliwala 1996).

This implies a symbiotic relationship between power and ideology, which gains expression and perpetuation through structures of all kinds — judicial, economic, social, and political. Empowerment in this framework therefore means a transformation in power relations. Specifically, it means control over resources (physical, human, intellectual, intangible); control over ideology (beliefs, values, attitudes); and changes in the institutions and structures that support unequal power relations.

Notions of citizenship, like institutions, are inextricably bound up with relations of power. 'Like power relations, citizenship rights are not fixed, but are objects of struggle to be defended, reinterpreted and extended' (Meer 2004, 32). The negotiation is around societal positions that discriminate against women, and gender roles (including the public/private divide that acts to contain women and their agency primarily within the private sphere, while opening men's agency to the public sphere). It is also around unequal power formed on the basis of class, caste, ethnicity, and other key markers of identity. Not only that: the negotiation is also a challenge to ideas that frame how we see the world and how we act.

Similarly, claiming rights is a political process, played out as struggles between the interests, power, and knowledge of differently positioned actors. A rights-based approach to development argues that all people are entitled to universal human rights, and development should be oriented to meeting those rights. A rights perspective politicises needs (Ferguson 1999). While a needs-based approach identifies the resource requirements of particular groups, a rights-based approach provides the means of strengthening people's claims to those resources. The challenge of the rights-based approach is 'in maintaining equal emphasis on the need to build both citizens' capabilities to articulate rights *and* the capabilities of political-economic institutions to respond and be held to account' (Jones and Gaventa 2002, 26). For individuals and groups, demanding accountability requires a sense that they have a right to do so (claiming that political space), and mechanisms through which their demands can be made and responded to. On the other side, accountability (according to the UNDP *Human Development Report 2000*) is judged by whether appropriate policies have been implemented and progress achieved.

Transformation: the role of development agencies

We think that transformative goals exist uneasily within large development organisations, as they are likely to be overcome by technical considerations more amenable to administrative practice. The key questions are: given the uneasy relationship between transformation and large organisations,

how can we strengthen the capacity of State and development bureaucracies to deliver on their operational mandates? And how can we shift organisational practice to focus better on equity and exclusion?

In order to strengthen the project of transformation, we need to disaggregate the range of strategies and activities that are dumped in the gender mainstreaming bag (such as policy reform, advocacy, capacity building, analytical frameworks, programme development, monitoring systems) and analyse their gains and their failures (Subrahmanian 2004). This should also help us to think strategically about what these institutions are well placed to do. At the same time, measurement systems need to be developed that can capture the full range of gender equality outcomes, both tangible and intangible.

Figure 2: Dynamics between top–down and bottom–up forces of change

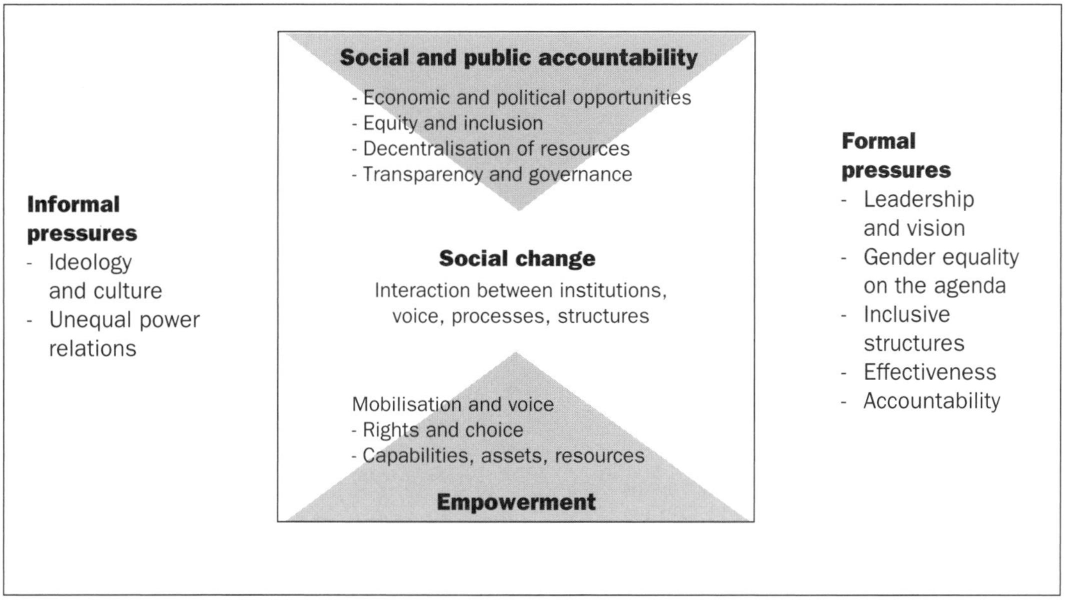

Informal pressures
- Ideology and culture
- Unequal power relations

Social and public accountability
- Economic and political opportunities
- Equity and inclusion
- Decentralisation of resources
- Transparency and governance

Social change
Interaction between institutions, voice, processes, structures

Mobilisation and voice
- Rights and choice
- Capabilities, assets, resources

Empowerment

Formal pressures
- Leadership and vision
- Gender equality on the agenda
- Inclusive structures
- Effectiveness
- Accountability

Our change strategies should envision *institutional* change. This does not mean reducing programmes such as those focused on education or women's entrepreneurship. It means seeing these not as ends in themselves, but as means to equality. Institutional change requires political activity to translate education or improved health care into equality. One important idea is that of working on both demand and supply sides of the institutional change equation. By the supply side, we mean shifting opportunity structures towards equality for women; changing incentives and capacity in global, State, and community agencies to respond to women. This includes delivering on services and on rights. On the demand side, we mean strengthening women's awareness of their own agency, voice, and mobilisation; their influence over institutions; and their ability to hold them to account.

Organisational deep structure

Organisational change needs to go far beyond policy adoption and large-scale processing of staff through gender training workshops. It is clear that, like any other complex skill, the evolution of knowledge and values (particularly for men) is a long process, requiring practice. Gender theme groups and specialists need to be better resourced, but more importantly, they need to be part of decision making. Even when senior managers agree that gender is important, gender equality still has to displace other important values in decision making. Only by ensuring a strong voice for gender equality advocates in decision making will gender concerns be represented in the day-to-day discussion of competing needs and values that are at the heart of development work. Numerous analysts have emphasised the importance of strong leadership and accountability structures, including performance appraisal and better monitoring. While we would agree that these are needed, 30 years of research and practice in the private sector shows that these 'command and control' strategies are not enough for significant organisational change.

In our work, we have described the 'deep structure' of organisations. Like the unconscious mind of individuals, this is largely unexamined, but constrains some behaviour and makes other behaviour more likely (Rao *et al.* 1999). The deep structure is the collection of taken-for-granted values, and ways of thinking and working, that underlie decision making and action. (See Figure 3.) Power hides the fact that organisations are gendered at very deep levels. More specifically, women are prevented from challenging institutions by four inter-related factors:

- **political access**: there are neither systems nor actors who can put women's perspectives and interests on the agenda;

- **accountability systems**: organisational resources are steered towards quantitative targets that are often only distantly related to institutional change for gender equality;

- **cultural systems**: the work/family divide perpetuated by most organisations prevents women from being full participants in those organisations, as women continue to bear the responsibility for the care of children and old people;

- **cognitive structures**: work itself is seen mostly within existing, gender-biased norms and understandings.

It should not come as a surprise to learn that the deep structure of most organisations is profoundly gender biased, and acts as a brake on work for gender equality. For example, one aspect of the deep structure is the separation between work and family. As Joan Acker pointed out, a key assumption in large organisations is that work is completely separate from the rest of life, and

Figure 3: The iceberg of organisational structure

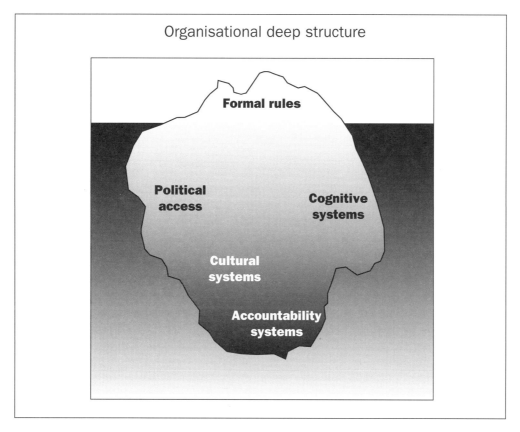

the organisation has first claim on the worker. From this follows the idea of the 'ideal worker', dedicated to the organisation, unhampered by familial demands, and… *male* (Acker 1990). Another aspect of the deep structure is the image of heroic individualism. As organisations were originally peopled by men, they are, not surprisingly, designed and maintained in ways that express men's identity. Heroic individualism can lead to a focus on winning, and noticeable achievement. This contrasts with the largely process-oriented, and sometimes long-term, business of understanding gender relations in a particular context, and acting for equality. In addition, given stereotypical gender roles, heroes tend to be men, further contributing to the idea of men as the ideal workers and women as 'other'.

Generating power to change organisations

We believe that there is a web of five spheres in which power can be generated to move an organisation towards transformation.[4] These five spheres are:

- politics;
- organisational politics;
- institutional culture;
- organisational process;
- programmatic interventions.

The political sphere

This is based on the assumption that because they live within gendered societies, few organisations will devote the time, energy, and resources to effective gender equality work unless pressured to do so. But is there a women's constituency that is exerting sufficient pressure for gender equality to be noticed by the organisation as an issue requiring attention? In some cases donors or boards of directors have been the source of some pressure, but local, political pressure has more potential for holding organisations accountable. The key skills required are organisation and advocacy. The pressure generated by this sphere may have many results, but they are dependent on work in the other spheres.

Organisational politics

This refers to the day-to-day bargaining that goes on between bureaucratic leaders as they struggle to make their particular views a reality. This sphere is about access of gender advocates to power, their bargaining ability, and skill in the use of power. Power is built from position, coalitions, clarity of analysis and purpose, and assets such as access to senior levels, and the ability to provide valued goods (information, technical expertise, material resources). The strong voice of an outside constituency is a tremendous asset, but far from all that is needed for a bureaucratic player. The outcome of bureaucratic 'victories' may be stronger policy, or increased resources, or even the evolution of an alternative organisational culture.

Institutional culture

Institutional culture is that collection of values, history, and ways of doing things that form the unstated rules of the game in an organisation. Most importantly, culture defines what is valued as being truly important in the organisation (often at odds with official mission statements). This sphere is important because of its capacity to make things happen as well as to block

them. Another way to describe culture is as organisational ideology: 'Ideology is a complex structure of beliefs, values, attitudes, and ways of perceiving and analyzing social reality — virtually, ways of thinking and perceiving' (Batliwala 1996, 2).

Culture then, can be a powerful ally in making work on gender equality a valued part of the organisation's work: the normal, the reasonable, 'just good development' (Rao et al. 1999). Similarly, culture can exclude — making the organisation difficult for women — and force a focus on 'harder', more 'real', outcomes (such as infrastructure projects). Cultures are generally changed by the influence of leaders, and by the understanding of others that the new directions are valuable.

Organisational process

This is the vehicle that turns the intangibles of bureaucratic politics, organisational culture, and political pressure into organisational action. This happens through programmes, policies, and services. The question is whether there are sufficient resources, and sufficient skilled and knowledgeable people, to lead the process of learning and change. Ultimately, knowledge must be spread through the organisation, and gender equality must become part of the organisational skill set, along with other aspects of development. If resources and expertise are the grease of organisational process, then approval mechanisms that require gender analyses are the drivers. For example, some development agencies require a gender analysis and strategy as a component of all projects. Finally, because gender equality has never been achieved, organisational learning needs to be seen as a key capacity. This leads us to work on the ground.

Programmatic interventions

These constitute the last (and first) sphere of power. It is here that the work of the other spheres is validated. It is also here that the organisation delivers value or not. In the

Figure 4: The organisational likelihood of promoting gender equality

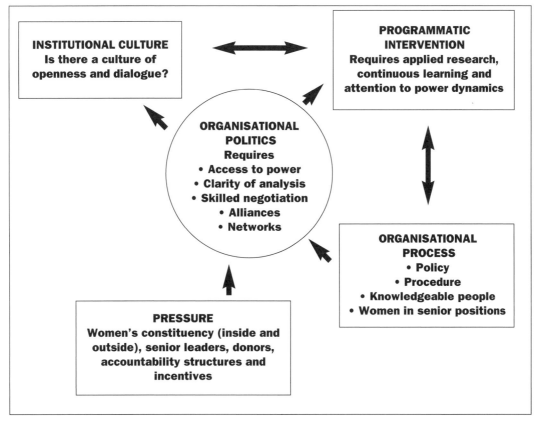

area of gender equality, what is of value is still contested. What used to be thought of as good practice is now challenged as insufficient. What this means is that this sphere must be energised by applied research, and by the development of new methodologies that can make a difference. These methodologies must also capture the attention and support of other parts of the organisation, as well as its partners.

Figure 4 shows some of the relationships between these spheres of power.

Even when the focus is at this level, however, we have reservations regarding the usefulness of organisational change strategies for making large organisations more interested in working towards gender equality. These strategies are helpful when managers feel strong and continued pressure to change. But in many cases, in large multilateral organisations, the pressure for work on gender equality is intermittent and muted. The difficulty with governmental systems is similar: seldom is there significant pressure to take gender equality seriously, and many government officials are in any case isolated from the pressure.

Building knowledge for transformation and a 'politics of solidarity'

In this article, we have argued that life after mainstreaming must be focused on institutional transformation. This envisions changes not only in material conditions of women, but also change in the formal and social structures which maintain inequality. Organisations must also be transformed, so that women's empowerment and gender equality are firmly on the agenda, and are supported by skilled, politically influential advocates. None of this will happen without the simultaneous creation of enabling environments (supply), and the mobilisation of women's groups for rights and access to power and resources (demand).

This vision is not the reality we now face. Our experience to date is telling us that there is a frightening lack of knowledge with which to accomplish the institutional changes we need. Parts of this knowledge do exist in the work of organisations in different parts of the world. We need to bring these pieces together, and forge a new set of understandings, which can guide our work beyond mainstreaming.

Finally, in these times of political and economic conservatism, gender advocates within development organisations, and feminists working in all kinds of spaces, need to come together to build what some have called 'a politics of solidarity'.[5] This is needed to infuse our work with vision and energy. A politics of solidarity can help us to assess strategically how to advance this transforming agenda, particularly when different political and institutional arenas are not working in synergy with our understanding of social change.

Aruna Rao is Co-Director of Gender at Work. She is a gender and institutional change expert, with over 25 years' experience of addressing gender issues in a variety of development organisations, primarily in Asia. She currently also serves as Chair of the Board of Directors of World Alliance for Citizen Participation (CIVICUS), and served as President of the Association for Women's Rights in Development (AWID) from 1998 to 2001. She holds a Ph.D. in Educational Administration from Columbia University, New York.

David Kelleher is Co-Director of Gender at Work. For more than 30 years, he has worked with non-government and public organisations, helping them build their capacity to further their social mandates. For the last few years he has been involved in a number of gender and organisational change projects. He has been a Fellow at the Simmons Institute for Leadership and Change in Boston. He has also been a member of the board of Directors of AWID, and is currently the Afghanistan, Pakistan, and Bangladesh Co-ordinator for Amnesty International (Canada).

Gender at Work (www.genderatwork.org) exists to build knowledge and capacity on strategic change for women's empowerment, gender equality, and social inclusion. It was created in June 2001 by AWID, Women's Learning Partnership (WLP), CIVICUS, and United Nations Fund for Women (UNIFEM). It works with development organisations and focuses on the links between organisations, gender equality, and institutional change.

Notes

1 Beijing Plus Ten is the UN-led ten-year review of the implementation of the Beijing Platform for Action, adopted by the Fourth World Conference on Women held in Beijing in 1995.

2 Gender at Work is a knowledge and capacity building organisation focusing on the links between gender equality, organisations, and institutional change. Gender at Work works with development and human rights practitioners, researchers, and policy makers.

3 This framework is adapted from the work of Ken Wilber.

4 This framework owes much to all the previous work in this field, but particularly to Graham Allison (1969) and Caren Levy (1996).

5 See for example Deniz Kandiyoti (2004).

References

Acker, J. (1990) 'Hierarchies, jobs and bodies: a theory of gendered organisations', *Gender and Society*, 5: 390-407

Allison, G. (1969) 'Conceptual models and the Cuban missile crisis', *American Political Science Review*, 63(3): 689-718

Batliwala, S. (1996) 'Defining Women's Empowerment: A Conceptual Framework', in *Education for Women's Empowerment*, New Delhi: Asia South Pacific Bureau of Adult Education

Elson, D. (2005) 'Section 1: Macroeconomics, well being and gender equality', presentation at a panel organised by UNRISD at The Ford Foundation, New York in March 2004, to launch the UNRISD publication *Gender Equality: Striving for Justice in an Unequal World*, 2005

Ferguson, C. (1999) *Global Social Policy Principles: Human Rights and Social Justice*, London: DFID

Goetz, A. (1992) 'Gender and Administration', *IDS Bulletin*, 23, Brighton: Institute of Development Studies

Goetz, A. (1997) *Getting Institutions Right for Women in Development*, London: Zed Books

Goetz, A. and S. Hassim (2003) *No Shortcuts to Power: African Women in Politics and Policy Making*, London: Zed Books

Hannan, C. (2003) 'Gender Mainstreaming: Some Experience from the United Nations', paper presented at a conference on Gender Mainstreaming — *A Way Towards Equality*, Berne, 20 June 2003

Jones, E. and J. Gaventa (2002) 'Concepts of Citizenship: A Review', *IDS Development Bibliography* 19, Brighton: Institute of Development Studies

Kandiyoti, D. (2004) 'Political fiction meets gender myth: post-conflict reconstruction, "democratisation" and women's rights', in 'Repositioning Feminisms in Development', *IDS Bulletin*, 35(4): 134-6, Brighton: Institute of Development Studies

Levy C. (1996) *The Process of Institutionalizing Gender in Policy and Planning: The Web of Institutionalization*, Working Paper No. 74, Development Planning Unit, University College, London.

Meer, S. with C. Sever (2004) *Gender and Citizenship: Overview Report*, Bridge Pack on Gender and Citizenship, Brighton: Institute of Development Studies

Millennium Project Gender Task Force on Education and Gender Equality (2005) 'Taking Action: Achieving Gender Equality and Empowering Women', www.unmillenniumproject.org (last checked June 2005)

Narayan, D. (1999) *Can Anyone Hear Us?* Washington D.C.: The World Bank

North, D. (1990) *Institutions, Institutional Change, and Economic Performance*, Cambridge: Cambridge University Press

Rao, A. and D. Kelleher (2002) *Unravelling Institutionalized Gender Inequality*, AWID Occasional Paper No. 8, Toronto: AWID

Rao, A., R. Stuart and D. Kelleher (1999) *Gender at Work: Organizational Change for Equality*, Connecticut: Kumarian Press

Sen, A. (1999) *Development as Freedom*, New York: Anchor Books

Sen, G. (2004) 'Remaking Social Contracts: Beyond the Crisis in International Development', Irene Tinker Lecture Series, International Center for Research on Woman, Washington DC, 16 November.

Subrahmanian, R. (2004) 'Making sense of gender in shifting institutional contexts: some reflections on gender mainstreaming', in 'Repositioning Feminisms in Development', *IDS Bulletin*, (35)4: 89-94, Brighton: Institute of Development Studies

UNRISD (2005) *Gender Equality: Striving for Justice in an Unequal World*, Geneva: UNRISD

Wilber, K. (1999) *The Collected Works of Ken Wilber*, Volume 4, Boston: Shambhala Press

Re-thinking gender mainstreaming in African NGOs and communities

Senorina Wendoh and Tina Wallace

This article examines research on gender mainstreaming initiatives, undertaken by a sample of local NGOs in four African countries. This research explores where resistance to gender equality comes from in some African organisations and communities. It shows that for gender mainstreaming processes to be effective they need to address the complex realities of people, and be sensitive to the values of communities in their implementation. The more successful gender mainstreaming initiatives have worked with local people's beliefs and realities, and allowed sufficient time for attitudinal change in both local people and NGO staff.

Transform Africa is a network of training and organisational development NGOs. It supports local African NGOs to develop their skills, and helps them to address some of the inequalities in their relations with NGOs from the North. The research discussed here grew out of the experiences of some of these NGOs. They were concerned about a perceived resistance to gender equality issues that they saw in some of the local NGOs they were supporting, and in the communities with which they worked. The research was undertaken by Transform Africa, in collaboration with the Transform network and supported by The Community Fund (now called The Big Lottery).

The main aims of the research were to understand the reasons for this perceived hostility towards gender equality in some African NGOs and those they worked with; to seek out African perspectives on gender and equality issues; and to share the findings widely to enhance understanding of what gender equality means in the context of different African countries.

The research focused on the communications, and collaborative work, between NGOs in the global North and South, and the communities with whom the latter work. Information was taken from local NGOs, partners, and communities in four African countries: Zambia, Rwanda, Uganda and the Gambia. The organisations included The Community Development Resource Network (CDRN) in Uganda, The Catholic Commission for Development (CCD) in Zambia, Programme Regional de Formation et d'Echanges pour le Développement (PREFED) in Rwanda, and African Consultants in The Gambia. In all cases the research was conducted by local researchers with the participation of Senorina Wendoh from Transform Africa.[1]

These are countries with contrasting economic, political, religious, and cultural contexts. Within each country, the range of experiences and findings included in the research comes from various rural and urban settings: settings which are more 'included' in the political mainstream, and those which are more marginalised. In each country, a Transform partner organisation undertook research with several of its NGO partners, and the communities with which they worked. In addition, some randomly selected NGOs they had not worked with before were included in the sample. All the NGOs said they were trying to work with gender issues, though few were specialist or women's NGOs.

The research made it clear how different the contexts are in different communities in the same country, and between countries, and that they were all undergoing rapid change. This change is occurring through environmental degradation, changing employment patterns due to globalisation, the growth of conflict, the spread of HIV/AIDS, and worsening poverty. NGOs and communities are living in fast-changing contexts in Africa, and many of the changes are out of their control.

It quickly became apparent that much work to address gender inequality is reaching local people through government initiatives. These are usually donor-promoted. The research findings indicate that gender mainstreaming is still largely an external concept. It has been adopted by governments and by some local NGOs, usually those headed by women and urban based. Gender mainstreaming is often perceived by other local NGOs to be for the benefit of donors, rather than for the benefit of communities. They find themselves grappling with ideas of gender equality that they have little understanding of, or ownership over. They feel that many of the ideas are imposed by those with power over them (their international NGO partners, donors, or government).

The 'foreign-ness' and lack of local ownership of the gender agenda often lead to different forms of resistance, including outright rejection, scepticism, or people masquerading as gender-sensitive, with no real understanding or appreciation of the issues. The research suggests that improving relationships and ways of working on

gender will enhance acceptance and implementation of policies and practices. Gender mainstreaming must therefore involve local NGOs and communities in the development of concepts, frameworks, and reporting formats, and these must be culturally rooted. They have to relate actively to the needs and realities of poor women and men. If there is no sense of ownership, it is unlikely that gender mainstreaming can be sustained at all levels of government and civil society, from central to provincial, and from district to local.

Furthermore, gender mainstreaming must contribute to women's empowerment, within both development organisations and communities, so that women stop being a target group and become active players in gender work. Too often they are seen as objects of development, rather than agents of change able to contribute to a transformation process that meets their own analysis and aspirations. It is not for external agents to determine what changes they need, or to tell them what roles they must play and what resources they need to access. Women must — with support — define and work for the changes they need. This will enable them to start to articulate, and gain access to, their rights.

The following sections share some of the discussions held by the Transform researchers with officials in government ministries and local NGOs, and with people in communities in the four countries. They show how the concept of gender equality is often either misunderstood or misinterpreted within development agencies and communities. All quotations are taken from the research.

Discussions with government officials

Many governments in Africa committed their countries to the Beijing Platform for Action in 1995, and agreed to the formulation of gender policies. For some this led to the creation of gender ministries, while other governments created focal desks in existing ministries. Women's caucuses in some parliaments increased the represent-ation of women's voices, and women's concerns were also raised by lobbyists and individuals, in committees focusing on legal affairs, governance, and human rights. Many dedicated men and women were involved in the development of government gender policies, and planning consequent action. Everything looked set to improve for the empowerment of women and the achievement of gender equality.

Resistance at government level

However, closer scrutiny began to tell a different story. Government officials cited significant resistance *'at implementation level where people give higher priority to other activities and they grade gender issues at a lower level because of misconception[s]'*.

At the heart of the perceived hostility to gender equality work as being 'foreign', 'threatening', and a plan to 'usurp men's power' is the sense that it is external and not relevant. Indeed, the approach is seen as misunderstanding the essence of African societies. Such views can be found inside governments, even while they openly espouse the need to work on gender inequalities. One senior government official expressed the problem:

'We are living in a changing world, nobody can resist the change even if we insist on the cultural practices… [W]e are acting in response to government policy to uplift women, the donors also demand that we involve women, but… the role played by the Nnabagereka [king's wife] has influenced the way we do our work. Most donors give us a condition to include at least 65% of the beneficiaries to be women; the government policy says one-third.'

This comment captures both the hope contained in gender mainstreaming initiatives and the challenge of implementing policies about which there is ambivalence. While donors want two-thirds of the main beneficiaries to be women, the government decided on one-third because of a fear that benefiting women will mostly exclude men. The discussions, even at government level, repeatedly raised the spectre of robbing men of their power and status, something seen as deeply threatening. Often government officials say this is apparent at local level during implementation; only a few admit that these concerns are often shared also at government level.

In a different country another senior official echoed these sentiments:

'The gender policy is important, yet at the operational level there is still a lot of resistance, people want to address gender but in your mind, you don't think gender.'

Another government official asserted:

'To change people's mind… [y]ou can sensitise and train but implementing is difficult. We try to be there at implementation. We participate in training as the mouthpiece of the Division — micro-issues must include gender. Using the strategic plan of action, we make sure that certain gender priorities are included. There is a lot of antagonism, so we always have to be present to give weight to our focal points. We ensure that we are present. It is a long way [to implementing gender mainstreaming].'

According to one director of a Ministry of Community and Social Services, an under-standing of culture is vital and yet very complex:

'There is a lot of misunderstanding and weakness on the part of cultural policy makers even though gender is a subject that is being addressed every day. We should have awareness on issues of gender and culture. These things should be portrayed in a positive light [if mainstreaming is to have impact].'

The concerns expressed above were repeated during interviews with line ministries in each of the four countries. At the core of the resistance seemed to be a concern that the concepts of gender were culturally inappropriate, that there was a direct threat to men and male power, and that these concepts were hard to implement because they were not well adapted to local realities on the ground. In translating them into practice the concepts were poorly understood, if at all.

The role of donor influence

Many of those government officials interviewed referred to the power, and yet contradictory nature, of donor influence in mainstreaming gender. Respondents indicated that donors make gender equality a condition across the board, without analysing or understanding the key gender issues in any given context. They thus underestimate the challenges of implementation, and their funding patterns (with short timeframes and tight targets) often make this work difficult. A director of one government organisation stated:

'I have not much I can do, mainly because I implement the project according to the donor conditionalities. I would for instance arrange for a meeting to sensitise both men and women, or even the families benefiting, but the budget only limits me to what is earmarked.'

Local NGOs share these frustrations. While donors make clear demands and often have defined expectations of the outcomes for work on gender, they do not understand well enough the contexts, the barriers, or the demands of working out ways to address these complex issues in practice.

One local NGO programme officer defined their relationship with donors around gender in this way:

'Donors listen to what we want, we give them our plan and they give us funds. But you know how difficult it is, sometimes some of them take long to approve our plan and we can only start when they give us the funding. The different funders give money at different times of the year so that accounting is on-going throughout the year. I wish all the programmes started all at once, but they [donors] take long and sometimes they are the ones who indicate when the programme will start.'

While government officials, and some local NGO staff, say they appreciate the role that donors have played in raising the issue of gender equality and highlighting the need to tackle women's exclusion and subordination, they have many concerns about the donor role. These include the fact that what gender inequality means in different contexts is poorly understood by donors, and the ideas are often not fully understood by staff responsible for implementing gender work. Donor procedures — with tightly framed budgets, timetables, and predicted outcomes — do not enable the kind of work needed for sensitive social and cultural change to take place effectively. Local NGO staff cannot control *how* they go about mainstreaming gender equality, because of donor conditions and demands. These are often applied in a blanket way across countries and cultures that are, in fact, highly differentiated and work in very different ways.

The gender mainstreaming conundrum among local NGOs

The challenges faced by government officials charged with the mainstreaming of gender approaches are also experienced by local NGOs who work to mainstream gender analysis and goals into their organisations and communities. Among those interviewed about addressing gender inequality in their work, there were far fewer success stories than stories of resistance encountered by the NGO workers.

Gender terminology and objectives have become a condition for funding among many donor agencies, including international NGOs. Therefore local NGOs — which always need money for their work and have few opportunities for raising funds locally — include 'gender' in their funding proposals. Sometimes they do this with little or no understanding, and often with little or no intention of using the funds for these purposes. A respondent in one country observed:

'Donors insist on gender in their funding activities, they cannot fund an activity unless there is a gender component.'

The result is that, often, proposals for funding incorporate a gender element solely to fulfil donor requirements, without any real commitment to mainstreaming gender in organisations or programmes. This donor-led insistence on including a gender element, without due regard for local perspectives, skills or analysis, results in NGOs masquerading as gender-sensitive at best, and becoming resistant, mistrustful, and sceptical at worst. This is how one respondent interpreted the funding conditions:

'Economic issues are one reason we take things from the outside because we are dependent on the north. We do not contextualise them. For example we have now adopted the international way of thinking that man must share power with the woman.'

The problem of rapid change

Also central to the challenge of gender mainstreaming is the speed with which the idea of gender equality has been adopted. Such a rapid adoption has meant that NGO staff and communities either do not believe in the idea and associated concepts, and simply 'parrot' the terminology, or they do not understand its significance. It is common to hear the English words 'gender main-streaming' dropped into many conversations at village level: presumably there are no local terms for it and people do not really know what the words mean. One male NGO director clearly expressed concerns echoed by many about the rapid manner in which mainstreaming was adopted by many governments and NGOs:

'Beijing was not a good thing because it was not sensitive to African culture. Bazungu [foreigners] come with their agenda and we swallow it whole without considering our own contexts. Bazungus come with their things from Beijing, and we take it automatically. It came at top speed and expected things to change overnight. People living in town copied it without considering the knowledge and habits of rural people. It was global, like a wave of thinking, a fashion, ideology that was very fast.

Everybody was uncomfortable with it but nobody talked about the discomfort. When Beijing came, some women reacted and went quickly. This led to conflict and divorce in families. Women from town and foreigners don't tell them the truth because men and women can't be equal. Some women reacted radically, others sceptically and others indifferently. The speed with which Beijing was adopted in the country, it threatened traditional structures, because "man is the chief and if you come with power, he resists".'

The above quotation reflects much of the hostility that many men who were interviewed for this research exhibited towards the concept of gender equality. Many men — even those expected to implement these approaches in local NGOs — were fearful, uneasy, and threatened by these new ideas and definitions, which challenged much that they had believed since birth. Many women, with less choice and control in their own lives, were also fearful about aspects of these gender concepts in discussion. In contrast, some women responded positively to concepts coming from Beijing. In particular these were the more educated urban women, who had some opportunities and significant choices in their lives.

The fact that NGOs are rooted in their own cultures means that staff reflect the gender relations prevalent in their society. They find it hard to combat these internally, as well as in their work with communities. The issue of organisational culture is therefore key to gender mainstreaming. The following quotation is taken from an interview with a male director of an organisation that considers itself gender-sensitive and which has conducted gender training. It shows the depths of the confusion that ensues when ideas are only half grasped and concepts applied inappropriately.

'But you cannot forget who a woman is because she cannot forgive anything, to put her as a manager she'll end up chasing all the workers... In the office I'm very gender sensitive because I employ a secretary she'll also make my tea, I'll tell her to do my filing, when I come when my *hair is not combed, she'll tell me, I write a love letter, she'll put it nicely on the computer — she's just like at home, some of the things my wife does, the secretary will remind me to look nice, to look clean.'*

It is unrealistic to work within short time-frames when the changes that are needed in knowledge and attitudes will take a long time, even generations, to achieve. Main-streaming gender analysis and practice is a process that requires changes to long-held cultural beliefs and practices. If they are to be effective, these changes must allow people to begin to see their value and develop owner-ship of the concepts and the change processes needed to implement them. Many NGO workers addressing gender issues complained of project and training time-frames that are limited. They allow little time for them to understand and change, and give them barely enough time to begin to work with communities:

'To change a person is a difficult thing. These olds, their minds are just in their culture. We tell them you expect things to change… Some have accepted but others have not. But I think if this thing goes on these youths will be better and better. They are now learning, it's just these old ones.'

Gender training workshops run by many local and international agencies are the key tool for gender mainstreaming. Yet this has led to levels of scepticism. Many NGO workers interviewed felt that one- to three-day workshops were not enough to challenge people's attitudes, or to under-stand the tools and frameworks that they were expected to use in their organisations and at community level.

One respondent acknowledged that he had attended a one-day gender workshop that was run by a government ministry. When asked what he thought about it, he said:

'A lot of noise. Women thought men were selfish and men thought women were interfering with their operations. I said to them "Justice is not to

bring gender balance but it is giving what is due to a person".

'The chief inspector of The Victim Support Unit [VSU] is a woman. She opposed what I said and I fought back to her and said the VSU is there to victimise men. When a man goes there to report maybe he is being abused by his wife, he is told to go and call his wife when she comes to tell her story, she is the one listened to and the man is locked up in the cell instead. Gender is a reaction against men.

'…Gender training brings theories people don't believe in, but since there are some allowances for attending, people go only because they are interested in them. After that, life continues. After the workshop, people laugh and tease each other and say to the women when they ask for a lift, "we are gender here, look for your own cars".'

The issue of attending workshops to gain the *per diem* allowance, rather than to learn new ideas, is a real problem for many organi-sations. It is, of course, absurd to try and change attitudes and beliefs about gender inequality, and to try to promote new ways of working through one-day workshops anyway.

Many of the struggles experienced by local NGOs with the rapid speed of mainstreaming, and the short-term training that is used as the main approach, are reflected in the interview below, with a woman project manager:

'On the surface it feels like all men and women have embraced the idea of gender. But maybe people act differently from the way they feel. They all seem to embrace the idea of gender, yet gender seems to be for women [in practice]. Every time there is a gender workshop, the men look at me or the secretary to be the ones to go. Why? Because we are women. It is happening everywhere in Rwanda even in government. A woman is the one who is chosen whether or not she knows anything about gender or even the language of the workshop [if it is in English]. It is as if gender is outside of them [men]. They have not yet internalised it. Why is preference given to women in projects [e.g. water and

sanitation], yet it is men who are invited to build the projects. This makes women to continue to be dependent because they do not know how the machines work, and are at a loss when the machines break down... At work and in organisations, women are always appointed as treasurers because they are trustworthy and do not steal, yet at home, women are not trusted to be in charge of finance or property. Many women live in rural areas and work in agriculture. They can't read or write, and there is need to train them. Those who have been able to learn are few.'

As noted earlier, NGO staff are rooted in their own socialisation and upbringing, and carry many gender concepts into their lives at work. Enabling them to analyse and explore their attitudes, and to see which ones might block the achievement of aims that they espouse, such as the alleviation of poverty, is a slow process and one that demands a range of responses, not simply short workshops. Inadequate attention is paid to working with staff on their own beliefs and practices. This ensures that they are ill equipped when it comes to explaining and training on gender issues in communities. Their lack of understanding is one source of real resistance. Another is the fear of the implications of gender equality work for themselves.

Communities and gender mainstreaming

In almost all the communities we encountered, elements of hostility and bewilderment about gender issues were expressed. The core concept that people did seem to grasp was that of 'gender balance', which we were told had 'been brought from Beijing', usually by the government. When asked what was meant by 'gender balance', many of the informants said it meant '50–50', or that 'women should be equal to men'. The concept of gender balance, in terms of numbers and equality, had been introduced to these communities through vigorous government advertisements and NGO workshops. Yet most men and many women, especially in rural areas, felt alienated and threatened by these ideas.

Religious faith and traditional cultural values are important in communities. These are not easily reconciled with the current concepts of gender equality imported from international agencies and donors. The Christian church as it exists in the research areas appeared to be even more resistant to change than African cultural values. A church official had the following to say:

'We respect women. These new foreign ideas are confusing our women. The bible states clearly that the woman is the priest in the home while the man is the priest in the Church. We honour them for the work they do in the home.'

While there is plenty of evidence of women being active in the Church, the research did not uncover any signs of this being a route to women claiming new rights or asking for change in their lives. The examples seen showed women playing a largely subservient role within the life of the Church.

Mainstreaming initiatives often fail to stress the strong link between gender inequality and poverty. The idea that women need to be able to access resources and take some control in their lives is not made clear, yet without this, the concept of equality risks alienating men. They feel their authority and position is being directly undermined, and they lack understanding of what the benefits of change might be.

One man expressed the resentment felt by many men in many communities:

'Beijing helped the country to adopt a law on gender. Before Beijing, men decided everything, even the life of women but now men can't do anything. They can't sell a land, cows, even TV without the agreement of the woman. [N]ow... the men fear the law... because it makes men feel bad, they feel that they are being forced to do things. According to the law, if men sell anything without consulting women/wife, the police will come and take you to prison: "it is as if Beijing came and diminished the power of men".'

Most gender mainstreaming initiatives also do not seem to take into account that in some contexts, men have the power to block changes:

> *'Authority belongs to the father. It is natural that children belong to the father. Because it is the man who marries the woman, he is also the one who takes care of the children, the one who names them and gives them away in marriage.'*

Another view was:

> *'I appreciate that women have been marginalised but I do not agree with the approach used to emancipate them. The whole movement has eroded our culture, women no longer respect their husbands not even elders. The process has been so fast with little consideration of our cultural values. When women get money for instance, they forget cultural norms. The whole question of women empowerment is not our culture, it has failed even in the west.'*

Furthermore, gender mainstreaming initiatives within communities do not properly relate to the perceptions and needs of the women. Outsiders, not insiders, define women's needs. Women are told what equality means, without first listening to them and assessing the realities and constraints of their contexts. Where women are entirely reliant on men, for example for access to land or protection for their children, talking to them about demanding rights within the family falls on deaf ears. Expecting women to confront social and cultural norms concerning divorce, child maintenance, inheritance, or violence — without understanding their own perception of what their needs are, and what they feel is possible — is unrealistic. What is appropriate about women's right to a livelihood or control of their bodies in one context does not necessarily apply or work in another. Even NGO workers, who often know these local realities and understand the language and cultural concepts, sometimes try to impose ideas that are alien and unhelpful. They do this in order to meet donor requirements, rather than working with their own

knowledge to help women to see what would be of real value to them in their current situations. Decisions are rushed; there is often not the time to discuss, raise issues and awareness, or challenge and introduce new ideas at a pace that women can understand.

The range of livelihoods open to women varies greatly in the different regions, as do the reactions of women: a wide range of views and opinions wase expressed in the research. In some contexts they are already breadwinners and relatively independent, while in others they are highly dependent in every way and cannot even begin to engage with ideas such as gender equality. The following reactions elicited from women in the four countries reflect the varying realities:

> *'We depend on men for our livelihood. We do not own land. Once I leave my father's home to get married, I cannot go back. I have to stay with my husband. If I leave him, where can I go? What will happen to my children?'*

> *'If my husband marries another wife, I cannot stop him. I don't mind sharing him because his new wife will help with tilling the farm. At least I have a home. I can't go back to my parents' home. There is no land.'*

> *'When my husband died recently, his mother and relatives arrived to inherit me. I chased them away. I was so angry — my husband had barely been buried, and they were doing this. What about AIDS? These people don't care for me or my children. I can take care of myself and my children. Even when my husband was still alive, I took care of this family.'*

> *'Many of the women are unhappy with the polygamous set-ups in their village. Their husbands do not help them to pay school fees for the children. Some men only sire children while only the women struggle with fees. They say they are oppressed in marriage… "What can we do? We can't take such matters to the Local Council, because the Local Councillors [an elected position equivalent to the village elders/chiefs] are themselves polygamous." They can't go back to their homes, because their*

fathers are also like that [polygamous]. There are more women than men. And women own nothing.'

The voices quoted above indicate that opportunities for change are very different in diverse contexts, and so there cannot be a blueprint. Even among people in the same country, there are differences based on rural/urban experiences and expectations, generation, literacy levels, access to resources, and land ownership.

Both women and men in local communities, especially where poverty is rife and opportunities are constrained, felt bewildered and uncertain about the introduction of concepts of gender balance and equality by governments and local NGOs. Change is ongoing all around them, and some are seeking certainty rather than further change and challenge. Others feel that the ideas as they understand them have no place in their communities. Those more able to embrace the ideas tended to be those with more economic options, and/or education and access to towns. Men were often hostile because they felt threatened, women were uncertain and confused because the concepts seemed so far removed from their daily lives and the problems they are grappling with.

From the local to the global: some local NGO progress in gender mainstreaming

'Yes, you expect resistance to gender because it is like you are against norms of customary law… definitely you expect them to resist. From our experience, what matters is approach.'

While the work of gender mainstreaming is still a huge challenge to many, some NGOs (the exceptions in the research, rather than the norm that was presented earlier) have achieved success. By beginning their sensitisation processes through their local leaders, using men to talk to other men, women to other women, and age group to age group, and by clearly demonstrating the value of according equal opportunities to

men and women, these local NGOs have made in-roads where government ministries are still struggling. They have found a way to tailor their approach to local needs, through listening and careful co-operation with local people. This is something that governments find hard to do, because gender mainstreaming is centralised and their messages tend to be universal and spread across the country in a uniform way.

Forming alliances with local leaders

Some local NGOs have found ways of building strong alliances with powerful local leaders. These may be political, religious, or traditional. This has meant it is easier to push the gender agenda forwards. Local leaders have themselves spearheaded gender equality work. Because most leaders are male, this approach has meant that other men have become allies, and they have in turn communicated the importance of gender equality to their fellows. Traditional meeting places, where local cases and matters of importance are discussed, have been appropriated as places for communicating the importance of gender equality and supporting such initiatives as inheritance rights for widows, the writing of wills, and the education of girl children:

'We go through the chiefs and headmen; we involve them and let them participate. They even contribute goats and chicken for the occasion and they feel part and parcel of the process. They also own it. Our workshops discuss the importance of human rights contained in the constitution, the law of marriage and divorce, inheritance, then gender and its link to poverty — what can be done, what has gone wrong. Finally we teach them on the law of inheritance and succession because it is controversial. We have gained a lot of experience from being down there with the community. We debate issues with communities… If I take you to the community, men will tell you now they sit down with their wives and women are also free to ask/challenge men and question positions in society. The husbands hesitate to beat their wives because the women say they'll take them to (our NGO).'

An official from another NGO explained the complex nature of gender mainstreaming, and how it is perceived differently at international and local levels:

'Talking about gender at an international conference is different from engaging with rural communities. National NGOs want to talk about gender to communities and it is like Greek, because they don't understand why women should change. You have to start from the known to the unknown. It is a big leap from the past into utopia. When you sit with communities, you must start from where they are, then talk about concepts.'

It is evident from the approaches discussed here that local NGOs can tap into issues and areas that are relevant to the local community and make progress on gender issues. They avoid using frameworks that can appear to be foreign, that can cause confusion or that risk alienating the people with whom they are working.

Conclusion

The research carried out by Transform Africa suggests that the challenges to successful gender mainstreaming are multiple. They include the speed with which gender mainstreaming has been implemented, its blanket approach to complex realities on the ground, standardised and quick workshops intended to change attitudes and practices almost instantly, short project timeframes, and approaches that have little impact because they ignore the processes required to change long-held beliefs and practices.

The few success stories uncovered by the research suggest that the seeds of change lie within the communities themselves. They are able and willing to analyse and think about their situation, and confront the need for change if the process starts from their own analysis and understanding. It is enhanced when leaders support the process and encourage change. This is often done by referring to times when women were more respected, and by highlighting the damage that current gender relations do to families, communities, and the work to tackle poverty. If a gender mainstreaming process is fully embedded within the communities, and takes the time to start from there — introducing new ideas and challenges in ways and at a pace that can stimulate and excite rather then threaten and demoralise — then it will be able to bring about change from within, rather than imposing it from outside. The challenge for donors, governments, and NGOs is to find ways to support and encourage positive change in favour of women, rather than bringing in blueprint ideas and concepts that have no meaning for local actors.

Senorina Wendoh has been involved in research on gender and poverty at the grassroots and was part of the Kenya Women Coalition's mentoring team during the Poverty Reduction Strategy process in Western Kenya. She is currently the Transform Gender Research Co-ordinator on 'African Perspectives on Gender'. She is based at the Transform Africa Office. Contact: Transform Africa, 4P Leroy House, 436 Essex Road, London NI 3QP, UK. smwendoh@aol.com

Tina Wallace has worked on gender issues in development practice for many years, and has written about the challenges in various articles and books. She is currently a Research Associate at International Gender Studies, Queen Elizabeth House, Oxford. Her current work involves researching relationships within the 'aid chain', and supporting the Transform research on 'African Perspectives on Gender', as well as working directly with NGOs, especially in Africa. Contact: International Gender Studies, Queen Elizabeth House, St Giles, Oxford, UK.

Note

1 Full country reports have been written. Contact Transform Africa for details: seri@transformafrica.org

Strategic gender mainstreaming in Oxfam GB

Elsa Dawson

This article[1] describes and assesses a strategy to mainstream gender issues in the South America region of Oxfam GB, both in its programme and in the organisation's internal systems and procedures. The experience shows that relating gender equality to strategic thinking is key to its effective incorporation into a programme. If staff do not see gender equality as a central part of what they are meant to be working on, they are unlikely to dedicate time to it. This depends both on managerial clarity and written plans.[2]

In 2001/2, Oxfam GB carried out a Gender Review for the whole organisation, which I co-managed together with the Oxfam Gender Adviser.[3] The aim of the Gender Review was to assess progress achieved in gender mainstreaming throughout Oxfam's programme, and within the organisation itself. Gender mainstreaming was launched as a worldwide strategy at the 1995 Beijing Conference, in which many Oxfam staff participated. For the Review, specialists were contracted who had expertise in gender analysis, combined with the various aspects of development in which Oxfam was involved, including humanitarian aid, advocacy on trade, and ensuring the integration of gender issues into poverty reduction strategies. The role of the specialists was to examine these programmes and draw conclusions regarding the extent to which working towards gender equality had been successfully integrated. The recommendations of the Review were translated into an organisational plan of action, and into regional gender mainstreaming strategies.

The plan of action proposed interventions in four areas: programme, leadership, learning and development, and knowledge management.

In 2003, I was asked by Oxfam GB's Regional Director for South America to design the gender mainstreaming strategy for her region. On her departure, I was asked to facilitate the implementation of the strategy, and I undertook this work as Regional Gender Adviser for the period July 2003 to April 2004.[4]

Gender mainstreaming: defining it for Oxfam GB

Various definitions have been drawn up, but the central idea with relevance to Oxfam is that, for an organisation committed to social action, gender equality should not just be the concern and responsibility of a few specialists, but rather an essential part of the work of all members of staff, as well as an integrated part of all organisational systems and procedures. It is therefore important that staff have a sense of ownership over the way gender concerns are integrated into their work.

Writing in an Oxfam publication (1999, 10), March *et al.* define gender mainstreaming as: 'To integrate gender concerns into every aspect of an organisation's priorities and procedures… Making gender concerns the responsibility of all in an organisation, and ensuring they are integrated into all structures and all work'. Oxfam defined gender mainstreaming in a set of guidelines for its staff as follows: 'A process of ensuring that all its work, and the way it is done, contributes to gender equality by transforming the balance of power between women and men' (internal document November 2002, no page number).

The phrase 'and the way it is done' refers to internal procedures and systems. Oxfam (ibid.) states that this process involves:

- recognising the links between gender inequality and poverty;

- assessing the different implications for women and men of its development, humanitarian, and advocacy work;

- devising strategies and systems to ensure that the different concerns, experiences, and capacities of women and men fundamentally shape the way in which all programme and advocacy work is planned, implemented, and evaluated;

- ensuring that Oxfam's internal practices are consistent with the above.

This definition does not clarify whether gender mainstreaming for Oxfam means a 'gender and development' (GAD) or 'women in development (WID) approach and associated activities. This important issue was left to staff in the regions to decide. Pialek (2004) suggests that gender mainstreaming is essentially about internalising a commitment to challenging inequality between women and men — a GAD

approach. He contrasts this with WID approaches which focus on satisfying women's practical needs without challenging gender power relations.

Hilary Standing (2004) takes a different view, observing that work which might be classed as WID in nature should be included in the way that gender mainstreaming is conceptualised. Although development and humanitarian programmes will effect more sustainable change if they do aim to correct power imbalances between women and men, an activity aimed at helping women in a practical way may well support them to redress power imbalances. An example is supporting women to earn more income, which meets both the practical need for more resources, and potentially enables them to meet their strategic need for greater power within the household. Including work which does not explicitly address gender power imbalances in the concept of gender mainstreaming enables staff to perceive the links between the improvement of women's daily lives and changes to gender power relations.

Oxfam's South America region

The South America programme is based in Lima, Peru. It implements development, humanitarian, and advocacy activities in Peru, Bolivia, Brazil, Colombia, Ecuador, and Chile, operating mainly via local non-government organisations. The programme concentrates on improving poor people's livelihoods, via direct interventions and lobbying on trade issues, urban poverty, assistance for indigenous groups, and humanitarian aid for victims of violent conflict.

Gender inequality remains a key factor in relation to poverty in the region, despite important gains by women in recent years, such as their increased role in community leadership. Women are still vastly outnumbered by men in local government, suffer higher rates of unemployment, and tend to be clustered in low-paid low-skilled sectors. Between 20 and 30 per cent of low-income households are headed by women. This number is rising in urban areas, and the incidence of poverty in women-headed households is greater than in those headed by men. The poorest women are located in the rural areas, where they are largely responsible for subsistence agriculture, which has been seriously affected by trade liberalisation. In urban areas, women outnumber men in the low-paid informal sector, and generally suffer from worse working conditions and lower remuneration than men. Many women work as household domestics, receiving inadequate pay and social protection. In all these areas, women have to balance their unpaid domestic responsibilities with income-earning activities, as South American men still largely refuse to do their fair share of domestic tasks, for fear of being branded unmanly. Even in the Lima Oxfam office, it was rare to see men serving refreshments at meetings; this was a task usually carried out by administrative-grade women.

An urgent issue throughout the region is violence against women, especially in contexts of conflict, where rape and sexual abuse are systemic. Domestic violence against women is also widespread, and ingrained in both women's and men's images of what it is to be masculine.

A gender mainstreaming strategy for South America

It was the Oxfam Regional Director's awareness of this situation, coupled with the organisation's gender mainstreaming action plan, which led her to contract me to develop a gender mainstreaming strategy for the region. Having worked in South America for ten years and for Oxfam's Programme Learning Team for another ten, I had a useful background for providing ideas about how this could be done.

An important consideration was how to develop a strategy which would be owned by key regional staff, especially the managers of the five country programmes, and which would inspire them and their staff to take action. Interviews were held with a selection of programme staff, including all country managers, to find out their opinions as to what progress had been achieved, what challenges remained, and what major steps were required to improve gender mainstreaming. Most importantly, they were asked to express their visions of a gender-mainstreamed society. What would this look like, from their perspective?

With regard to progress already achieved in mainstreaming gender, it was clear that the majority of staff had good levels of understanding and capacity in relation to gender analysis, and that regional leadership was clear that addressing the gender power imbalance was a priority for the region's poverty reduction effort. There were also many examples of effective gender mainstreaming in the programme. However, these tended to follow a WID approach; not specifically directed at addressing gender inequality, although in practice they may have done, as observed above. Programme objectives rarely included mention of working towards gender equality, and gender analysis was largely absent from contextual poverty analyses.

The overall vision from regional staff for a gender-mainstreamed region was that it should represent a strategic contribution to the achievement of more equal relationships between men and women in South America. The major challenge was how to ensure that gender equality emerged from the realms of rhetoric and was translated into real changes in women's lives. They hoped the region would provide Oxfam with a South American perspective on gender equality, taking into account the multicultural, social, and ethnic context of the continent, and that regional budgets would reflect Oxfam's seriousness regarding gender equality in the distribution of resources. In the workplace, they aspired to a place where each person felt 'empowered', respected, and appreciated for their professional capacities, with a reasonable balance between male and female staff numbers at each level.

Integrating gender equality into programme activities

Activities proposed had to be feasible within the schedules of busy programme staff, and make sense in terms of the contexts in which they were working. The gender mainstreaming strategy designed to achieve this vision focused on strategic 'acupuncture points'. These were key areas where introducing specific changes in the way the regional programme was managed would really make a difference in terms of the organisation's ultimate impact on gender inequality. It was therefore proposed to:

- develop gender and power analysis to support the regional programme;

- use the conclusions to develop corresponding objectives which expressed Oxfam's intentions related to gender equality;

- support this with an effective staff training programme in gender sensitivity.

The importance of integrating gender sensitivity at all stages of the programme management cycle was emphasised, i.e. throughout situational analysis, design, implementation, monitoring, and evaluation. It was observed that there was not much point adding in gender concerns at the implementation or monitoring stages if it was not there in the analysis and design. How poverty relates to gender inequality needed to be explored from the start, otherwise it was unlikely to be addressed by the programme's objectives or activities, and key interventions likely to address poverty would be lost. For example, in livelihoods programmes, women may become overburdened with more work, rather than having their workload alleviated; or areas where low-income women's employment is clustered may be missed in a programme

aimed at improving working conditions. Once such aspects have been analysed, the programme can prioritise them, recognising the central role that reducing gender inequality plays in poverty reduction in the planning stage.

Minimum standards were designed for the integration of gender analysis into programme proposals. Oxfam uses an electronic programme-management system and database, with facilities for monitoring indicators and impact. For each section of this format, indications for the inclusion of gender considerations were drawn up and agreed on by each country programme manager, to be used by staff as they designed their programme proposals. The compliance of staff with these standards was to be the subject of a review in June 2005, led by regional management.

As Oxfam largely relies on partners to carry out analysis at the programme level, some changes in the portfolio of partner organisations were necessary, so that Oxfam would be working with more organisations capable of providing effective gender analysis. It proved difficult to select new partners, especially where long-term relationships had been built up with specific partners. In some areas, there was a more restricted choice of partners. For example in the Andes fewer agencies existed, especially those with high level capacity for gender analysis. I suggested some alternative organisations for country managers to consider, and one of these suggestions was taken up.

Internal organisational procedures

In terms of internal organisational procedures, a key action was to include in the personal performance objectives of all programme staff the aim of ensuring that a gender perspective was built into the programme. It was hoped that this would lead to every manager monitoring the performance of every staff member, in terms of gender mainstreaming, during every performance review. The capacity to carry out gender analysis was also to be made a key criterion for the selection of all new staff, although in practice staff were still taken on without this capacity. Induction packs included information on the importance of gender equality for Oxfam, and how the organisation incorporates a concern for it into its work. Job descriptions made clear the responsibilities of the post regarding main-streaming gender. All new regional managers were to demonstrate passion, enthusiasm, and understanding regarding gender equality and its relationship to poverty issues in the region. The new Regional Director recruited at the end of my contract certainly appeared to fulfil this criterion. A gender lead was also to be appointed with sufficient time and resources to implement the gender main-streaming strategy, with the support of gender focal points in each country office. My role as Gender Adviser encompassed that of gender lead for the ten months of my contract, but as I was not replaced and it was decided not to appoint the country focal points in each office, the implementation of the strategy suffered.

Administrative staff were made aware of Oxfam's position on gender equality and women's rights, and the relationship of this to the organisation's ways of working. A workshop for all regional and Peru office administrative staff was held. During this workshop, examples of the links between women's inequality and poverty, such as the high percentages of women-headed house-holds among low-income groups in the region, were explained. This convinced many initially doubtful staff members of the importance of introducing a gender analysis into the programme's conceptualisation. Male participants were given the job of serving the refreshments!

Learning and development

A gender learning and development plan was designed, focusing on key areas that staff identified, given their importance for the development of the regional programme in the context of South America:

- gender and the macro-economic situation;

- gender and indigenous/*mestizo* culture;
- gender and humanitarian work;
- gender and violence;
- gender and participation;
- gender and urban issues.

Learning exchanges were to be organised between beneficiaries, partners, and Oxfam staff. These would use external specialists in each area to facilitate learning, as a way of supporting all these groups to develop their understanding in a mutual fashion, without Oxfam making claims to be the expert and pushing a particular agenda. An electronic distance-learning programme was also proposed on the above six themes, using the Internet and electronic discussion forums to bring together specialists and staff located around the world. This would be related to and complemented by distance-learning programmes. It was intended that staff should dedicate seven hours a week to these programmes, which would include:

- CDs of learning materials;
- electronic essay exchanges;
- series of one-day seminars;
- electronic debates and discussions.

Other proposed means of learning were:

- a register of local sources of gender training;
- support for staff to attend training courses;
- leaflets with key information about how to mainstream gender;
- sharing a list of useful Internet links and bibliographies;
- exchanges with academic staff;
- collaboration with doctoral students who wish to implement participative research and document Oxfam experience.

Box 1: Novib's 'traffic lights' criteria

These criteria are divided into three phases, which are likely to represent the progressive development of an organisation in terms of capacity for implementing gender-sensitive development programmes.

Phase 1

- Gender-disaggregated baseline monitoring, evaluation, and impact information is collected, analysed, and used to inform programme development.
- Female and male beneficiaries participate equally in decision making in planning, implementation, and evaluation of projects, and their voices are reflected in the way programme decisions are made.
- Staff and volunteers have a sufficient level of understanding and skill to enable a basic gender analysis and gender-aware approach to be carried out.

Phase 2

- A rights-based gender analysis that demonstrates the links between poverty, discrimination against women, and gender inequality is developed, and this analysis is reflected in the organisation's policy and programme.
- There is a balance of women and men in senior and middle management, or the organisation is actively seeking to redress an imbalance in order to reflect more equitably its beneficiary population.
- Women and men understand the need for gender-balanced decision making and are able to ensure that decisions taken reflect their different interests.

Phase 3

- A significant number of male staff members and beneficiaries are actively engaged in work to strengthen gender equality.
- The organisation actively exchanges knowledge and information, collaborates with others to extend and share its learning on gender issues, and uses this learning to shape its programme.
- The organisation challenges gender-stereotyped beliefs and discriminatory attitudes towards women, both in its internal practices and externally.

Source: Oxfam 2002

The planned model for learning and development, based on mutual learning activities, was envisaged as a model that the region could use to support learning in other areas. It was developed in line with plans for global learning being promoted by Oxfam's Programme Learning Team. However, these plans were not carried through into the region, which had no general learning and development strategy in place at the time. The interim regional management team found the gender knowledge development plan too ambitious, and decided it should not be implemented.

Working with partners on gender mainstreaming

A monitoring and support tool was developed for staff to work with partner organisations on gender mainstreaming, based around the programme management cycle. The 'traffic lights' criteria for monitoring gender integration in partner organisations, developed by Novib Oxfam Netherlands (see Box 1), were used as a way of identifying partners who had weak capacity related to gender analysis and gender-sensitive programming. This was tried out in Ecuador, where partners were asked to identify the tasks they carry out, or felt they should carry out, in relation to gender equality at each stage of their programme management cycle. The agreed actions were to be monitored in future visits by Oxfam programme officers. A workshop was held with Intermón (Oxfam in Spain, who took over the Ecuador programme from Oxfam GB), and other Oxfam International[5] members, to agree overall gender mainstreaming strategies and ways of working to ensure this work continued.

Knowledge management

In order to improve knowledge management in relation to gender, it was proposed that each office should appoint a gender focal point who would be responsible for receiving and distributing information regarding gender, and supporting staff to use it. Annual impact reports would be used for identifying gender mainstreaming success stories, and how achievements were made. These would then be transmitted to staff via the South America Intranet site or the electronic bulletins being planned. The gender focal points would also promote the gender learning and development plan. However, this was not carried through; again it was considered too ambitious and there were concerns that country offices lacked the capacity to appoint the focal points.

Major issues arising from the strategy

Ownership and the need for 'rooted' gender analysis

Nicholas Pialek and I wrote gender analyses for staff on key regional themes: livelihoods, conflict, and urban issues. However, despite condensing these into succinct three-page summaries, they were not widely used. Pialek (2004) observed that the livelihoods gender analysis came to conclusions which conflicted with the analysis generally held by regional programme staff, and was therefore not accepted by them. For example, whereas the gender analysis cited evidence

of how trade liberalisation had benefited women by providing them with new employment opportunities, the trade advocacy was focused on lobbying against free trade *per se*, rather than looking for ways to modify its effects on women and men.

If this gender analysis had been part of the original analytical exercise on livelihoods, the contradiction which arose between the gender analysis and the programme analysis would have been resolved as part of the process of arriving at conclusions. If Oxfam's poverty analyses generally took into account gender concerns, and the interests of poor women, they might come to different conclusions which would lead to better interventions from the perspective of disadvantaged women. However, the speed with which programmes have to be designed in Oxfam usually means that social analysis (and within that, gender analysis) is not sufficiently deep.

This experience taught us that it is insufficient just to *provide* staff with analyses — they need to develop these themselves in order to take them on board in their planning and programme management. It begs the question of how this can be done effectively, given the shortage of time. My experience suggests that it can be done in three ways:

- selecting staff already possessing appropriate gender analytical knowledge regarding the contexts in which they will be working; or

- providing staff with learning and development opportunities on the job; or

- ensuring that programmes are implemented only with partners who have the appropriate knowledge and skills.

Competing priorities for implementation staff

A major problem in implementing the strategy was that staff at all levels felt they did not have time to participate in it. Pialek

(2004) points out that the confusion around the degree of priority given to gender equality results from Oxfam's dual strategic approach. On the one hand this states the need to mainstream gender throughout the organisation's five strategic objectives; and on the other hand makes gender equality an objective on its own, and the last one at that. This dual approach allows staff to see gender as an add-on, leading them to say it is not their priority, rather than seeing gender sensitivity as an integral part of the management of a high-quality programme. For example, I was asked not to approach one significant programme in the region, so as not to 'overburden' the manager. Instead, my intervention could have been seen as potentially helpful to her.

It was therefore key that gender equality be explicitly part of agreed programme objectives, as stated in the programme proposal minimum standards, so that staff and partner organisations would see this as part of their work, rather than as an add-on.

Who does the gender analysis?

Carrying out regional-level analyses was a lengthy activity, demonstrating that this is not an easy task, but requires resources and analytical capacity. The gender analyses developed by Pialek were appreciated by regional management, but some of his key conclusions were not accepted by staff. The problem with using external help is that staff do not develop ownership of the ideas. This means that Oxfam either has to recruit staff who have the analysis skills in the first place, or give them the opportunity to develop the skills themselves.

Partner organisations are best placed to carry out a local gender analysis, given their first-hand contact with beneficiaries. But, unless their primary focus is women's issues, they have little time and capacity to carry out the analysis that a programme requires. Ownership of gender analysis is key, however. Many Andean-based organisations rejected Oxfam's policy on gender equality, describing it as based on Western

concepts of gender difference and relations. In this region there are indigenous societies where women are relatively equal to men, such as the Shipibos of the Peruvian Amazonian rainforest (Heath 2005). Staff were unable to communicate Oxfam's concern that even where gender equality might traditionally be less of a problem, an awareness of gender difference was still important. In overall terms in the South America region, unequal gender relations unduly affect women rather than men. This is particularly so as the encroachment of Western socio-economic processes have tended to make women more unequal. For example, Andean women speak less Spanish than men, which makes it more difficult for them to access markets as the markets are becoming increasingly Spanish-speaking.

The gender mainstreaming process needed more information regarding the different forms of gender relations among indigenous Peruvians, in order to judge whether the approach to gender equality being promoted by Oxfam needed modifying. A seminar on gender and ethnicity was planned to explore these issues and reach conclusions regarding what a South American concept of gender mainstreaming should look like. Some staff, for example, expressed concern that Western gender analysis fails to give value to the relations of complementarity and reciprocity, which are so much part of the Andean people's survival strategies. Woodford Berger (2004) also finds that 'the assumed oppositional positions of women and men in the social, economic, political and ritual order' (69), which is the basis of gender analytical frameworks, did not match the reality of people of Dormaa in Ghana. We failed to find a way in Oxfam's South America programme of communicating the possibility that gender could be about complementary relationships, possibly because of this essentially oppositional nature of the concept which Woodford Berger notes. However, in a strategic planning session for women involved in a Peruvian women's movement, I successfully used the metaphor of a Peruvian dance to encourage participants to visualise their ideal of gender relations, in terms of positive and complementary relations between the sexes.

Conclusion

The Regional Director was insistent on the importance of addressing gender inequality throughout the Oxfam programme through a gender mainstreaming strategy. However, the implementation of the strategy suffered as a result of her subsequent relocation to another region. Much less was achieved than was hoped for, demonstrating how crucial leadership is for successful gender mainstreaming.

The way that gender equality relates to strategic planning is key to its effective incorporation into a programme. If staff do not see gender equality as a central part of what they are working towards, they will not dedicate time to it. This depends both on managerial clarity and written plans. No amount of advisers, gender mainstreaming strategies, and gender training workshops can convince staff to mainstream gender if achieving gender equality is not a clear goal set out in their strategic plan. If this is then reflected in their personal performance objectives, and seen by them as an essential part of what they are expected to achieve — constantly reiterated by managers as important — the rhetoric may be translated into the reality of the programme and the lives of those it is intended to benefit.

Gender equality should also be rooted in the context of the programme. Research on positive achievements in mainstreaming gender shows that success is more likely where contextual preconditions exist (Beall and Todes 2004). Regional programme strategies could, for example, identify positive trends in relation to gender equality into which Oxfam can insert its efforts. The successes of women community leaders in El Alto, Bolivia, or those involved in the Lima community soup-kitchens movement, could be built upon to seek their greater representation at local political levels, currently still a gap in South America.

Another key lesson from this experience is that it is crucial that staff and partners carry out their own gender analysis, so that they own this and incorporate it into their way of thinking about the reality they intend to address with their programmes. If this is not done, staff will either reject the analysis, or merely pay it lip service without thinking through the implications for the details of their programmes. Their capacity to carry out gender analysis depends on the successful implementation of learning and development work related to gender.

Gender mainstreaming therefore needs to happen at the highest strategic decision-making levels in the organisation. Only then will staff be clear that working towards gender equality is an essential part of what Oxfam expects of them, and only then will they feel able to incorporate it into their busy work schedules.

Elsa Dawson has worked for twenty years in UK development agencies, both in South America and based at their UK head offices. She is a specialist in gender mainstreaming, and programme management, particularly strategic planning and evaluation, and currently works as an independent consultant in these fields. Contact: elsalouise@msn.com

Notes

1 An earlier version of this article in Spanish was accepted for publication by the review *Debates en Sociologia* produced by the Peruvian Catholic University of Lima.

2 Oxfam has worked on gender issues as a concern in their own right since the founding of a specialist Gender and Development Unit in 1984 (see Porter, F., I. Smyth, and C. Sweetman (1999) *Gender Works: Oxfam Experience in Policy and Practice*, Oxford: Oxfam).

3 I am grateful to Judith Flick for commissioning the design of the Oxfam South America gender mainstreaming strategy.

4 I was assisted in this task by Nicholas Pialek, a Master's student from the Oxford University Department of Development Studies.

5 Oxfam International is a family of agencies with similar aims, located in a number of developed countries throughout the world.

References

Beall, J. and A. Todes (2004) 'Headlines and head-space: challenging gender planning orthodoxy in area-based urban development', in 'Repositioning Feminisms in Development', *IDS Bulletin* 35(4): 43-50, Brighton: Institute of Development Studies

Heath, C. (2005) 'Looking Inwards: What Can We Learn from an Analysis of the Traditional Designs of Shipibo Women?', MA dissertation, Oxford

March, C., I. Smyth, and M. Mukhopadhyay (1999) *A Guide to Gender-Analysis Frameworks*, Oxford: Oxfam GB

Oxfam (2002) 'Gender Mainstreaming Tools', Oxford: Oxfam GB

Pialek, N. (2004) 'Gender Mainstreaming in Oxfam: Policy, Practice, and Institutional Change', Thesis presented at the University of Oxford

Standing, H. (2004) 'Gender, myth and fable: the perils of mainstreaming in sector bureaucracies', in 'Repositioning Feminisms in Development', *IDS Bulletin* 35(4): 82-8, Brighton: Institute of Development Studies

Woodford Berger, P. (2004) 'Gender mainstreaming: what is it (about) and should we continue doing it?', in 'Repositioning Feminisms in Development', *IDS Bulletin* 35(4): 65-72, Brighton: Institute of Development Studies

NGOs, gender mainstreaming, and urban poor communities in Mumbai

Vandana Desai

This article focuses on gender mainstreaming in small grassroots NGOs in the Indian city of Mumbai. It identifies some of the gaps in activities and challenges that these organisations face, and explores the links between gender mainstreaming and women's empowerment. NGOs working at community level can play an important role in supporting women to challenge customs, ideas, and beliefs which perpetuate unequal gender relations. This role of NGOs becomes particularly challenging in a context of rapid social and cultural change, such as Mumbai. The article argues that despite commitments to gender mainstreaming, NGOs have insufficient understanding that they can facilitate the process of empowerment of women in such a context.

Urban NGOs can strengthen the capabilities of women in slums, and can play a role in encouraging or inhibiting empowerment processes. Because of this, it is important to explore how NGOs can support women through rapid and dramatic economic, social, and political change. The article is based on information which was collected for a study of 67 grassroots urban NGOs and their operations (funded by the British government's Department for International Development). The NGOs on which the research focused are involved in a broad spectrum of service-delivery activities with a high profile and a strong tendency towards policy advocacy. Beyond this they exhibit potentially illuminating contrasts in emphasis and packaging, as well as in client group and organisational style (Desai and Preston 2000; Desai 2002).

This article draws on information from the research to explore several questions. How is a concern for gender inequality addressed by different urban NGOs? Which activities have been successful in supporting women's empowerment[1] and transformation of their social roles? What implications does the commitment of NGOs to work on gender have for feminist agendas?

The first survey for this research was carried out in 1995–6. In 2003, 40 of the NGOs were revisited, to see how their style of operation was evolving in response to economic and political changes. This follow-up was funded by the British Academy.[2]

The context

NGOs in Mumbai are working in an environment of rapid economic and cultural change. The Indian government's economic liberalisation policies have led to the privatisation of health, education, and other services to urban populations in low-income areas. In a context like Mumbai, public services have always been inadequate, but economic liberalisation has worsened the situation in many ways.

Poor women's aspirations have been dramatically affected by the impact of global economic change on urban life in Mumbai, especially after economic liberalisation in 1991 (Desai 2002). Many women have found opportunities in different industries that have developed since that date: for example, export-oriented manufacture of garments, jewellery, embroidery, and leather goods; but also service-oriented industries such as catering, beauty parlours, call centres, and computer/IT-related industries. These industries all demand a young, female workforce, whose attributes include a high level of skills — and in particular manual dexterity — eagerness to learn, a high level of commitment to securing and keeping employment, and a willingness to work long hours for low wages.

NGOs in the research reported that the young women in the urban slums of Mumbai who have greater opportunities for employment tend to be from comparatively better-off families, and have relatively high levels of education. In my conversations with young women in slums, they told me of their career plans, which were markedly different from those of older generations of women. Many of them were choosing not to work as domestic help in middle-class homes, which was the only option formerly available.

The social impact of this entry into employment is interesting. Young women are expected to share their income with their families. Yet, despite taking up employment and making financial contributions to household livelihoods, young women are still expected to work in their traditional roles within the home. NGOs reported that many women face conflict with relatives, because of the need to juggle their role in the new economy with their responsibilities to the family. But despite the extra workload, earning an income has led many young women to feel that they have greater freedom in movement and leisure activities, and an enhanced participation in household decision making. This was revealed by Sudha, a young woman to whom I spoke in a slum in Chembur:

'I go to work and bring money into our house, so that we can buy various things for our house. I can decide with my husband how we can spend our money within the household budget, while my sister-in-law stays at home and looks after the house and cooks our meals'.

All NGOs in the sample reported an increase in social problems, as a result of the new employment possibilities for women.[3] Young women's changing opportunities and attitudes are perceived negatively by older generations as resulting in feelings of superiority, which undermine existing social relations between the sexes and the generations.

Other young women from comparatively worse-off backgrounds are unable to take up new employment opportunities. They may lack an education, since household economic crises (often created by men's loss of employment) can result in children being taken out of school. School drop-outs have to search very hard for a means of making a living. One key survival strategy for women in the absence of alternative livelihood opportunities is to sell sex. A growing number of young women are working in the ever-increasing number of bars in the deprived areas of Mumbai. Many of these are sex workers, in the guise of waitresses. Some families depend on women migrating to other areas to work as sex workers. Away from home, nobody knows them. Associated with these trends are increased trafficking of women and children into sexual slavery, and increased rates of HIV infection.

Many NGOs report growing evidence that the degradation of living conditions in poorer households, and the day-to-day frustrations, have translated into an increase in levels of domestic and sexual violence, in which women are the first victims.

Renegotiation of identities

It can be seen from the account above that traditional views of what women do in the family are being undermined, and this is leading to radical and rapid change in poor women's lives. New ways of living are evolving, as gendered patterns of work change in both the formal and informal sectors of the urban economy. As these economic changes take place, women in the Mumbai slums are being exposed to fresh ideas and values, which oblige them to re-evaluate social identities and roles. Changes in the labour market and crises in urban livelihoods associated with economic globalisation are making poor urban women reassess their sense of who they are, and what they can do.

When I asked one woman about how gender equity could be achieved, she emphasised the need to redistribute roles and responsibilities, to allow women to work for a decent wage outside the home. This would require men to share more equally in the domestic, parenting, and caring activities within their household. This practical arrangement, she stressed, would save women time and hence increase their earning power. Ultimately it would increase household well-being. Another interview with young women in the slums of Mumbai illustrated their resistance to parental expectations relating to marriage, contradicting traditional expectations about arranged marriage. For example, one girl said,

> 'I will choose my own husband, try and know the person well before I get married, I don't care what other people think or my parents think, I have to live with him, if things go wrong nobody will help me, there is no point crying later' (Desai 2002, 221).

This reassessment of women's and men's roles and identities is, for many women, the first step towards challenging gender inequality.

The response of NGOs

NGOs have an important role to play in supporting women, men, and households so that they cope with these rapid changes in their lives and expectations. NGOs are increasingly being required to meet the welfare needs of women, men, and children living in poverty in the slums of Mumbai. The government is keen to enter partnerships with NGOs in projects to reduce urban poverty. In addition, it hopes that such partnerships will help to strengthen community organisations, in line with its aim of good governance and decentralisation. Decision making on many issues affecting low-income urban dwellers has now been devolved to the Mumbai Municipal Corporation, which is responsible for local government in Mumbai. The Corporation has reduced funding for delivery of health and education services, and NGOs working in partnership with it have moved away from their former role in service delivery to women.

Counselling and support services

Many NGOs are providing counselling and support services for married couples, (including spouses from different religions), parents, young people, and children. They offer a range of different kinds of counselling and support, including guidance on marriage and divorce; anger management, especially for young people; working to relieve stress; counselling on sex and sexuality issues; career guidance; and counselling for single-parent families and carers of elderly people.

Awareness raising and advocacy

Since service provision to urban communities has been cut back, households and communities have been encouraged to meet their own needs. Hundreds of thousands of urban dwellers in Mumbai have yet to see large-scale slum improvements under the Slum Redevelopment Authority in Mumbai. Mumbai generates approximately 6,000 metric tons of garbage every day.

NGOs report that more funding is available for awareness raising and information provision to enable individuals, households, and communities to address their immediate needs, than for direct service provision. Some mass-awareness programmes on health, hygiene, and clean environment target women, since they have particular responsibilities for these concerns within the existing gender division of labour. Educational awareness programmes are undertaken by NGOs like Stree Mukti Sangthana to encourage recycling, separating wet and dry waste, and the introduction of the concept of zero garbage.

SPARC (The Society for the Promotion of Area Resource Centres) offers an example of how women's immediate practical needs can be met alongside more transformative work to raise women's awareness of gender inequality. Sheela Patel, the director of SPARC, told me that that SPARC's strategy of providing women with skills, support, and resources to participate in a more formalised intervention to provide low-cost housing has increased women's self-confidence. From the mid-1980s, women have worked together to stop evictions, and to build and strengthen slum organisations. The aim is to demonstrate to governments and international agencies that women and men living in urban poverty can design, build, and manage projects to improve their housing, and to improve infrastructure and services.

An aim of many NGOs providing health and sanitation education is to transform women's awareness of gender inequality. Instead of focusing on service delivery or the delivery of technical information only, NGOs with a commitment to social transformation are now raising awareness among poor people about equality, social justice, gender sensitivity, secularism, communal harmony, and human rights. They aim to support people to influence policies and encourage political and social reform. The hope is to enable people to achieve a sense of entitlement to equal treatment in matters of human concern, to develop the capacity to reflect on their situation and to question this, and to take action.

To do this, NGOs in Mumbai have been using non-formal means of education through various media, including songs, role playing, street dramas and skits, informal meetings, and group discussions. Multidisciplinary forums are engaged in producing plays and films on current concerns, and television plays an important role in disseminating information. Rag pickers are targeted by Stree Mukti Sangthana, which provides them with some direct services (such as crèche facilities), and some information on important gender-related issues, such as reproductive health. Drama has been developed, such as *Mulgi Zali Ho* (A Girl is Born), a drama which highlights the inequality and discrimination a girl faces from birth to old age. Another is *Hunda Nako Ga Bai* (Say No to Dowry), which highlights social problems associated with the system of dowry. It is entertaining and often humorous, and attracts large audiences, including men.

The aim of such work is to raise women's and men's awareness about gender inequality, and to support women to learn to exercise their rights as citizens. This involves promoting their ability to speak up for themselves, and to protest if they are unfairly treated. It also involves women gaining understanding of their relationships with their wider communities, and challenging inequality.

Legal aid

The provision of legal aid by NGOs has increased, particularly by gender-oriented NGOs through forming a 'legal cell' which gives advice and guidance on various matters such as domestic violence, child abuse, matrimonial disputes, inheritance rights, Muslim women's rights, and the legal options which are open to resolve disputes. NGOs including *Majlis* (meaning Association), and the Forum Against Oppression of Women, have initiated campaigns for legal reform, to help women gain access to the legal system, and to counter the existing norms of gender bias within court structures.[4] They are also working to make women aware of their legal rights. These NGOs are lobbying policy-making bodies (through public meetings, seminars, media advocacy, and networking among activist groups, judiciary, government officials, and members of legislative bodies) to make the legal machinery more accessible to dis-advantaged poor people, and more sensitive to the needs of women. Their activities include conducting gender-sensitisation programmes for members of the judiciary, court functionaries, and the police.

Microfinance

In recent years, NGOs have played a key role in the provision of microfinance, targeting women in particular. This has, in many cases, contributed to women's economic independence from the household. More broadly, it has been asserted by some to lead to an increase in women's self-confidence, and their social standing. However, one study of the Grameen Bank and BRAC (the Bangladesh Rural Advancement Committee) highlights the fact that challenging gender relations potentially places women at risk, at least in the short term. One man in the study explained that 'our wives would not be beaten so much if they were obedient and followed our orders, but women do not listen to us and so they get beaten often' (Schuler *et al.* 1998, 151). Where a woman faces increased violence in the home, it is human nature to use avoidance strategies, such as docility and compliance, to solve the problem, rather than confront it and aggravate further violence. Consequently, an adverse reaction to changing identities has inhibiting impacts on empowerment processes. Such issues highlight the importance of maintaining a deliberate and strategic control over subtle and public displays of resistance.

NGOs, their activities, and the empowerment of women: 1994–2003

From the samples of NGOs surveyed in fieldwork, (67 in 1994 and 40 resurveyed in 2003), about a third were picked out and identified as either weakly or strongly gender-oriented. These categories focused on the types of activities undertaken by the organisations, with strongly gender-oriented NGOs undertaking the more transformative types of work.

The data collected covered, among other things, staffing, funding, and activities. The gender-oriented NGOs were found to be larger and growing faster than others, particularly those regarded as 'weakly' rather than 'strongly' gender-oriented.

This was true with regard to growth in numbers of paid staff. Nineteen NGOs had recorded staffing information in both years. Of these, in 2003, gender-oriented NGOs had an average of 58.5 staff, compared with 28.4 in other NGOs. However, most of the growth was accounted for by para-professional staff (that is, community members trained and employed to work for the NGOs in the community). In the gender-oriented NGOs, 42.5 out of the average 58.5 staff were paraprofessionals, while in the others, 16.4 out of the average 28.4 staff were paraprofessional. In the women-oriented NGOs, the number of staff had grown since 1994, by an average 22.4 staff (of which 21.7 were paraprofessionals), whereas in the others the average growth was only 2.4 staff (of which 1.4 were paraprofessionals). Thus, the gender-oriented NGOs had grown in terms of staffing far more over the ten years than other NGOs, but most of these were not professional staff.

A similar growth pattern was evident in terms of funding. In 1994, numbers of funders were similar between gender-oriented NGOs and others. All had around 3.5 funders each. But by 2003, gender-oriented NGOs had acquired the support of a further 2.8 funders each on average.

Interestingly, most of this growth was concentrated on the more weakly gender-oriented of the women's NGOs. Other NGOs which were not focused on gender had attracted only an average of one funder each.

Translating social relations perspectives into effective action

Alongside this growth in size of all NGOs there was also a broadening of scope, with gender-oriented NGOs expanding the number of activities undertaken more rapidly than others. By 2004, a particular focus on gender and social awareness programmes and legal-aid provision could be seen.

NGOs in Mumbai have been quick to absorb the new discourse and language of empowerment, participation, and governance, and the language of women's empowerment and gender equality. Most NGOs had replaced the word 'women' with the word 'gender' by the time of my second field trip in 2003–4. Some NGOs argued that this was a way of resisting any focus on gender inequalities. This is interesting since it was obviously far from the intention of the first proponents of gender and development, who argued that this actually led to a much more political focus than had been possible in women in development work (Moser 1993). For these NGOs, the word 'gender' meant integrating women into development activities along with men. Feminist agendas were unaddressed, despite the fact that the NGO staff interviewed emphasised that their organisation and individuals now have a greater recognition of the importance of social relations and power, and reform of policy processes and institutions. They are clear that they have moved on from an earlier focus on individuals (women, people in poverty) and development activity at the local level only. However, their analysis of gendered power relations does not appear to lead them to conclude, as many feminist analysts do, that the core issue is to challenge gender-based

discrimination in the distribution of power and resources.

These changes in policy focus seem to have had little effect on the lives of women living in urban poverty. The success of projects and interventions in Mumbai in addressing gender inequality was usually evaluated merely by counting numbers of women participants, rather than identifying changes or outcomes that have had a positive impact on gender relations, or reviewing unexpected results.

The challenges for NGOs

Many NGOs and government agencies today agree that it is important to invest in women since they are critical for economic growth and poverty reduction. Some of these understand that gender inequality needs to be challenged to enable women to participate equally with men. However, redistributing power in social relations and challenging male privileges in economic, social, and cultural life is a long, difficult, and uneven process. It is commonly assumed that NGOs are aware of problems generated by cultural transition and social transformation, and are capable of responding to these. Yet a number of challenges confronted NGOs participating in my study. The general impression from the research was that many NGOs had adopted a commitment to gender mainstreaming without knowledge and understanding of power relations or a commitment to combating gender inequality. I found that they were mainly dealing on a reactive basis with social problems that were emerging, and providing services to vulnerable women.

The popularity of gender issues as a donor-led agenda

I feel that the sudden interest in 'gender' from NGOs is not in response to demands made by women in slum low-income communities, but is donor-driven. As more funding is available for provision of credit programmes which have become successful and popular, NGOs have increasingly focused on credit programmes targeted at women. This is also in response to the Indian government's wish to be seen to be doing something on the Beijing Platform for Action.

The research suggests that NGOs in Mumbai have little conceptual understanding of how their interventions facilitate women's empowerment in the context of rapid economic, social, and cultural change. This change is constantly taking place in communities and neighbourhoods in which these NGOs work, and its processes have their own momentum. Both wider changes, and the planned development interventions which cut across them, are fragmented and *ad hoc*. Evaluation of impact is a challenge in such contexts. My experience of working with NGOs suggests that they rarely evaluate their interventions in the context of the wider economic, social, and cultural changes to which they respond (Desai 2002).

Challenges of organisational change
Working on gender issues, both within NGOs and with individuals, households, and communities, is a resource-intensive process that takes up time, energy, commitment, and financial resources. A particular challenge to organisations is that changing attitudes and norms is a very slow process.

My research suggests that even the most comprehensive approaches to institutionalising gender do not adequately emphasise the importance of organisational change, particularly organisational norms and culture. Providing incentives and accountability systems for mainstreaming gender is very difficult, as cost and efficiency considerations override concerns for more gender-aware, participatory practice. The latter is time-consuming, as it involves changing culture (discussed above), and as such, demands courage and innovation (see Goetz 1997).

Gender-sensitive development work is very dependent on particular NGO staff as individual agents of change. While most staff in bigger NGOs have had gender training, this should not be seen as a magical strategy for bringing about change. Instead, conscious effort must be made to change NGO structures and practices.

Differences among women
Staff of some NGOs said they had found that gender analysis tends to homogenise women's experience. However, differences exist between women in poor urban areas and these differences require a nuanced response. Time and again, NGOs emphasised their difficulties in addressing gender-based inequalities as these are affected by class, religion, ethnicity, age, location, and other particularities in different neighbourhoods of Mumbai. It is the heterogeneity of women, and their multiplicity of identities, that make it difficult to unite urban poor women as a political constituency. Most NGO staff and practitioners referred to women and men as homogeneous interest groups. This over-simplifies complex realities (see Murthy 2004). Even when there is recognition of different interests in communities, there is a tendency to underestimate the complexities of conflicts and negotiation at this level.

The question of difference between women is particularly important in the context of widespread use of participatory planning methodologies, which have been adopted extensively in many gender-oriented NGOs. Many NGOs involved in my research asked me how participatory development initiatives could address the complexities of urban poor communities and their differences based on age, wealth, occupation, religion, caste, ethnicity, and gender. There is a widespread assumption on the part of many involved in development that urban poor communities in Mumbai live in harmony. However, this is not the case. Local powerful elites dominate, and the more powerful groups can simply ignore inconvenient views. Participatory planning in this context is favouring the opinions and priorities of those with more power and ability to voice their views publicly. The complexity of this problem is further increased by many urban poor slum dwellers' pursuit of contradictory interests at different times. In my view, people's motivation to be involved in externally initiated participatory development processes has not been given enough attention (see Desai 1995).

Challenges of 'scaling up' grassroots work

Supporting vulnerable, excluded women and allowing their experiences, priorities, and needs to drive mainstreaming processes is not easy. NGOs require a high degree of honesty, courage, and commitment in forging alliances with other NGOs, donors, and social movements at various levels, from local to global. Yet there is a problem with scaling up effective work with women in poverty. Most participatory initiatives in my study were limited to localised, small-scale activities, and attempts to co-ordinate such successful participatory actions into larger more powerful movements had not been successful.

Conclusion

Development interventions need to be founded in an understanding of the social and cultural impact of globalisation and economic change in India, and how they are changing the nature of women's roles and participation in civil society. How is women's role and status changing with the passage from a traditional, religious society to a modernised, globalised society? How are women's expectations and aspirations changing? What 'subtle strategies' (Scheyvens 1998) are they employing to respond to the challenges they currently face? Within this context we need to gain a true understanding of processes of change, and improve our understanding of the linkages between livelihoods and various formal and informal institutions at the grassroots.

A much broader and more comprehensive approach is needed, to ensure that a commitment to challenging gender inequality is institutionalised within NGOs. Currently, it seems that many efforts to change policies, practices, and procedures continue to be frustrated by the wider social and economic dynamics that reproduce inequitable relationships between men and women. The first step is to understand women's local, informal, and qualitative day-to-day experiences of economic globalisation and its social and cultural impact. How global processes are affecting particular communities, especially women and their role within transitional societies; which aspects of the culture and social institutions are changing; and what these changes mean for women: these are all important issues to understand.

There is also a need to develop new techniques to monitor and evaluate these processes, especially as there has been little impact from anti-poverty interventions in many urban cities in developing countries. These analyses could feed into NGO action on women's experience of globalisation — both the considerable losses and the undeniable gains — to ensure that international laws and regulations work for women in poverty rather than against them.

How exactly can NGOs strengthen the capabilities of urban poor women, seeking self-empowerment? NGOs need to evolve a support system which does not just concentrate on individual struggles and strategies to achieve empowerment, but also focuses on collective gender concerns. NGOs should in future build relationships with feminist movements and be open to change in their own organisational culture, structure, systems, and procedures at the grassroots level.

Vandana Desai is Senior Lecturer at the Department of Geography, Royal Holloway, University of London, Egham TW20 OEX. Email: v.desai@rhul.ac.uk

Acknowledgement

I am grateful to all the NGOs who gave their valuable time during this research, to the Department for International Development and British Academy for funding the research, and to Caroline Sweetman for developing this article.

Notes

1 Here I mean empowerment as a fluid and often unpredictable process, which leads to fundamental social transformation of society that enables individual women and marginalised groups to make decisions that allow them control over their lives (see Scheyvens 1998; Parpart et al. 2002).

2 The aim of the study was to evaluate the transition in the style of NGO operation in the context of liberalisation and globalisation; to evaluate if NGOs are effective agents of civil society; and to assess how their role is developed in the context of the good governance, decentralisation, and democratisation agendas set by international donors and the World Bank.

3 This is also highlighted in Kelly's (2000) research in Manila, Philippines.

4 Along with matrimonial disputes and penal remedies in situations of domestic violence and child abuse, in recent years courts have focused increasingly on more challenging areas of economic rights, property settlements, the right of residence in the matrimonial home, and civil injunctions which would protect women against violence and abuse. The aim is to re-negotiate the spaces within the justice delivery system on women's terms, demystify statutes and procedures, and spread legal literacy.

References

Desai, V. (1995) *Community Participation and Slum Housing: A Study of Bombay*, New Delhi/London/Thousand Oaks, California: Sage Publications

Desai, V. (2002) 'Informal politics, grassroots NGOs and women's empowerment in the slums of Bombay', in Parpart *et al.* (eds.) (2002)

Desai, V. and I. Preston (2000) 'Urban grassroots non-governmental organisation in Bombay: a suggested typology', *Environment and Planning C: Government and Policy* 18: 453-468

Goetz, A.M. (1997) *Getting Institutions Right for Women*, London: Zed Books

Kabeer N. (1994) *Reversed Realities: Gender Hierarchies in Development Thought*, London: Verso

Kelly, P.F. (2000) *Landscapes of Globalization: Human Geographies of Economic Change in the Philippines*, London: Routledge

Murthy, R. (2004) 'Organisational strategy in India and diverse identities of women: bridging the gap', *Gender and Development* 12(1): 10-18

Parpart, J.L., S.M. Rai, and K. Staudt (eds.) (2002) *Rethinking Empowerment: Gender and Development in Global/Local World*, London: Routledge

Scheyvens, R. (1998) 'Subtle strategies for women's empowerment: planning for effective grassroots development' *Third World Planning Review* 20(3): 235-53

Schuler, S.R., S.M. Hashemi, and S.H. Badal (1998) 'Men's violence against women in rural Bangladesh: undermined or exacerbated by microcredit programmes?', *Development in Practice*, 8(2): 148-57

Resources

Compiled by Kanika Lang

Publications

Repositioning Feminisms in Development (2004) Andrea Cornwall, Elizabeth Harrison, and Ann Whitehead (eds.), IDS Bulletin, 35(4),
Publications Office, Institute of Development Studies, University of Sussex, Brighton BN1 9RE, UK. Tel: +44 (0) 1273 678269; fax: +44 (0) 1273 621202
g.edwards@ids.ac.uk
www.ids.ac.uk/ids/bookshop/index.html

This book emerged out of a workshop organised at the Institute of Development Studies in 2003 entitled 'Gender Myths and Feminist Fables: Repositioning Gender in Development Policy and Practice'. It provides a multi-authored perspective on the current challenges of feminist engagement with development as a transformative, political project. Authors return repeatedly to the question of how and why gender is such a depoliticised aspect of development today and what ideas about gender have become rooted within mainstream development organisations. Part One examines the ways of thinking about gender (gender myths and fables) that have come to be embedded within gender and development advocacy and programme work. Part Two looks at development organisations and their changing constructions of gender, and policies and frameworks to deal with inequality, and articles evaluate the different efforts at gender mainstreaming. Finally, Part Three presents challenges faced by international feminist engagement with development today i.e. how to position 'older debates on a new political canvas'.

Gender Equality and Men: Learning from Practice (2004) Sandy Ruxton (ed.)
Oxfam GB, Oxfam House, John Smith Drive, Cowley, Oxford, OX4 2JY,UK
www.oxfam.org.uk/publications

This collection of articles draws on the experience and knowledge of organisations like Oxfam GB. It focuses on the issue of working with men on gender equality to explore how this can be used to promote broader gender equality and poverty reduction strategies. The focus on men reflects the increasing recognition that it is crucial to involve men in any examination of their privilege and power in order to change gender relations that disadvantage women. The articles discuss experiences of working with men in diverse areas such as gender-based violence, sustainable livelihoods, and sexual and reproductive health. They include case studies from all over the world including Mexico, Yemen, the Caribbean region, and East Timor.

Gender, Development and Diversity (2004)
Caroline Sweetman (ed.)
Oxfam GB, Oxfam House, John Smith
Drive, Cowley, Oxford, OX4 2JY,UK
www.oxfam.org.uk/publications

This collection of articles looks at the implications of diversity and differences (in, for instance, gender, race, class, and age) for development organisations and their goals of poverty alleviation and human rights. Articles discuss the importance of multiple identities — based on class, age, and ethnicity, that intersect with gender — to determine the degree to which individual women identify with other women. The articles look at implications of this for development organisations which aim to mainstream gender, promote collective ways of working among women, and support women to challenge gender inequality. Case studies come from India, Zimbabwe, Uganda, Latin America, and the UK.

'Whose voices? Whose choices? Reflections in gender and participatory development' (2003) Andrea Cornwall, *World Development*, (31)8: 1325-42
www.elsevier.com

This article raises issues that are central to gender and development concerns. It discusses the extent to which 'gender-aware' participatory development initiatives really are participatory. It also questions the ability of such methods to represent the many cross-cutting and conflicting interests within communities. Cornwall argues against homogeneous categories of 'women' and 'men', and the current slippage between 'gender issues' and 'women's needs'. She emphasises that in order to be truly participatory, development interventions have to be sensitive to categories of difference held by the communities themselves, rather than imposing external and stereotypical categories of gender. Interventions also need to ensure that the voices of both

marginal women and men are provided with the space to be heard. The author stresses that the presence of women is important, but hearing the voices of particular women does not mean that all women's interests are represented. A crucial question she raises is: what happens when the needs that women prioritise are considered by the development organisation to be detrimental to their 'empowerment'? The author concludes that it is important to move beyond the assumptions that all women identify with gender issues, and that the process of bringing about change is a zero-sum game in which women-in-general are pitted against men-in-general.

'Institutions, organisations and gender equality in an era of globalisation', Aruna Rao and David Kelleher in *Women Reinventing Globalisation* (2003) Caroline Sweetman and Joanna Kerr (eds.)
Oxfam GB, Oxfam House, John Smith
Drive, Cowley, Oxford, OX4 2JY,UK
www.oxfam.org.uk/publications

This article builds on Rao and Kelleher's previous work on gender equity and organisational change, to offer a new approach entitled 'institutional change for gender equality'. The authors argue that organisations must address and change institutional rules, i.e. societal norms and values that determine the distribution of power, resources, and responsibilities, in order to make progress on achieving gender equality. Rao and Kelleher acknowledge the importance of a 'gender infra-structure' (e.g. an organisational gender policy), and organisational change (organisational learning and development to achieve gender equality internally). However, they stress that significant and sustainable advances towards gender justice will occur only if organisations challenge and change social institutions and rules that determine the distribution of power and resources between women and men.

Mind the Gap: Mainstreaming Gender and Participation in Development (2003) Nazneen Kanji, International Institute for Environment and Development (IIED) and IDS. IIED, 3 Endsleigh Street, London WC1H 0DD, UK. Tel: +44 (0) 20 73882117.
info@iied.org
www.iied.org

This paper provides an overview of the shifts from Women in Development (WID) to Gender and Development (GAD), and from participation to governance. The author argues that shifts in one field are mirrored by the other, in the focus on social relations, policy processes, and institutions. The paper provides a brief discussion of the similarities and tensions between the two fields, as well as a few thoughts on the means of bridging the gap between the two, through efforts such as renewed alliances with emerging movements.

Gender Mainstreaming: An Overview (2002) United Nations Publications, 2 United Nations Plaza, Room DC2-853, New York, NY 10017, USA. Tel: +1 212 963 8302; +1 800 253 9646; fax: +1 212 963 3489
publications@un.org

This brief UN booklet aims to tackle the lack of understanding about how gender perspectives can be identified and addressed. It starts with an explanation of what gender mainstreaming means, and stresses that the ultimate aim of the strategy is to achieve gender equality. It lists some basic issues and questions that can provide a starting point for thinking about differences between women and men. The final section discusses how gender can be mainstreamed into different contexts such the policy analysis, research, technical assistance and data collection, analysis, and dissemination.

Men's Involvement in Gender and Development Policy and Practice: Beyond Rhetoric (2001) Caroline Sweetman (ed.) Oxfam GB, Oxfam House, John Smith Drive, Cowley, Oxford, OX4 2JY, UK
www.oxfam.org.uk/publications

This book draws on a seminar of the same name convened in 2000 by Oxfam GB with the Centre for Cross-Cultural Research on Women. The contributors respond to two key questions: In what sectors and contexts should gender and development work involve men as beneficiaries? What issues face men who work in activities which have a commitment to gender equality and/or a feminist perspective? Authors draw on experiences from Nicaragua, India, the UK, Egypt, Nepal, and Lesotho to argue that gender and development theory, in practice, means not only working with women, but also working with — and for — men.

'Questions of power: women's movements, feminist theory and development aid' (2001) Signe Arnfred, in *Discussing Women's Empowerment: Theory and Practice*, Sida Studies no.3
www.sida.se/Sida/articles/10200-10299/10273/studies3_.pdf

Arnfred critiques gender and development and gender mainstreaming, arguing that a major constraint is that feminist scholarship has become integrated into government and development institutions and has lost its political edge. According to the author, WID and GAD discourses obscure the fact that tranformative feminist trends do exist in the North, and not all have been engulfed by what she calls 'development feminism'. She argues that a big challenge for women's movements is the need for 'reversals of learning', with feminists from the North listening to and learning from feminists from the South.

Institutionalizing Gender Equality: Commitment, Policy and Practice. A Global Source Book (2000) Henk van Dam, Angela Khadar and Minke Valk (eds.)
Royal Tropical Institute, KIT Press, PO Box 95001, 1090 HA Amsterdam, The Netherlands. Tel: +31 (20) 5688272; fax: +31 (20) 5688286, and Oxfam GB.
kitpress@kit.nl
www.kit.nl

Case studies in this book are drawn from Latin America, South Asia, and Africa to highlight different strategies used by development agencies and NGOs to mainstream gender into their organisational policies, planning, programmes, and structures. The diverse techniques discussed include the establishing of specialist gender teams, creating gender-sensitive work environments, building staff capacity, creating support for gender sensitive programmes and policies at all levels of staff and management, and gender training. The book also includes a bibliography and web resources section on the gender policies and programmes of different organisations and agencies.

Mainstreaming Men into Gender and Development: Debates, Reflections and Experiences (2000) Sylvia Chant and Matthew Gutmann
Oxfam GB, Oxfam House, John Smith Drive, Cowley, Oxford, OX4 2JY,UK
www.oxfam.org.uk/publications

This report provides a good overview of the arguments for why it is important to include men in any attempts to mainstream gender, redefine gender relations, and achieve equality between men and women through development interventions. The authors emphasise that a focus on men should not result in a diversion of resources from women (a central concern for opponents to men's inclusion). However, they also highlight the benefits of breaking the inaccurate association of gender with women, ensuring that women

alone do not have to shoulder the responsibility of transforming gender relations. In addition they stress the greater potential for sustainable change when men are 'men-streamed' in gender and development planning, policies, and programmes.

Feminists Doing Development: A Practical Critique (1999) Marilyn Porter and Ellen Judd (eds.)
Zed Books, 7 Cynthia Street, London N1 9JF, UK.
www.zedbooks.co.uk

Women from the North and the South engaged in development projects and critiques of development bring to light the challenges facing those with a feminist agenda in development. Section One explores the official structures that constrain feminists doing development, while Section Two lists the efforts of feminists to make projects more feminist. Sections Three and Four provide a more global perspective on feminist action and alliances, as well as the global forces that impact on feminist agendas in development.

Gender Works (1999) Fenella Porter, Ines Smyth, and Caroline Sweetman (eds)
Oxfam GB, Oxfam House, John Smith Drive, Cowley, Oxford, OX4 2JY,UK
www.oxfam.org.uk/publications

This book brings together 36 contributors to look at the efforts of, and challenges for, Oxfam, in putting its gender policy into practice. The authors draw on their own experiences as past or present staff of Oxfam in different regions of the world to provide insights into the implementation of Oxfam's gender policy. They discuss aspects that have worked and those that have been less successful in the context of gender-aware programme and advocacy work, organisational culture, and procedures. Case studies draw on experiences from Bosnia, Ethiopia, El Salvador, UK, Uganda, Burkina Faso, Pakistan, Cambodia, and the Middle East, among others.

'The evaporation of gender policies in the patriarchal cooking pot' (1999) Sarah Hlupelike Longwe in *Development with Women: Selected Essays from Development in Practice. A Development in Practice Reader*, Deborah Eade (ed.)
Oxfam GB, Oxfam House, John Smith Drive, Cowley, Oxford, OX4 2JY,UK
www.oxfam.org.uk/publications

The author examines why gender policies, so enthusiastically embraced by development organisations in policy statements, vanish by the time they reach the implementation stage. She analyses how bureaucracies responsible for development (both Northern agencies and Southern governments) can play a major role in the perpetuation of patriarchy. Likening development agencies to 'patriarchal cooking pots', Longwe explains how gender policies 'evaporate' from the policy articulation to implementation stage, through the use of a diverse range of tactics including policy dilution, lip service, tokenism, and subversion.

Gender at Work: Organizational Change for Equality (1999) Aruna Rao, Rieky Stuart, and David Kelleher (eds.)
Kumarian Press, 1294 Blue Hills Avenue, Bloomfield, CT. 06002 USA. Tel: +1 (860) 243 2098; orders tel: +1 (800) 289 2664; fax: +1 (860) 243 2867.
sales@kpbooks.com
www.kumarianpress.com

The fundamental premise of this work is the interconnectedness of gender inequality, organisational culture, and organisational impact. The authors argue that gender inequality is rooted in the 'deep structure' — i.e. the unquestioned values, history, culture, and practices of an organisation — which governs its work and impact in the wider world. Therefore, an understanding of, and a commitment to, gender equity must be entrenched within the culture of an organisation if it is to be attained in its external engagement and work. Drawing

on in-depth case studies from development organisations such as Bangladesh Rural Advancement Committee and commercial corporations such as the Body Shop, this book presents strategies for transforming organisations in order to work towards gender equality both internally and externally.

Feminist Visions of Development: Gender, Analysis and Policy (1998) Cecile Jackson and Ruth Pearson (eds.)
Routledge, Taylor and Francis, 2 Park Square, Milton Park, Abingdon, Oxford, OX14 4RN, UK. Tel: +44 (0) 20 7017 6000; fax: +44 (0) 20 7017 6699.
www.routledge.com

This collection of academic essays re-examines development through a gender lens and challenges unquestioned gender assumptions and concepts in development. The relationship between women and poverty, education and status change; gender interests and interests stemming from other forms of social identities (e.g. class and race) are all scrutinised. Other concepts under consideration include macro-economic policy, the household, industry, reproductive rights, feminism/s (including ecofeminism), and gender itself.

Missionaries and Mandarins: Feminist Engagements with Development Institutions (1998) Carol Miller and Shahra Razavi (eds.)
Intermediate Technology Publications, Intermediate Technology Development Group, 103/105 Southampton Row, London, WC1B 4HH, UK.
orders@itpubs.org.uk
www.developmentbookshop.com

The articles in this book describe the implementation of gender-equitable practices within development institutions, including state bureaucracies, multilateral organisations, and non-government organisations. Authors look at the strategies of, and challenges for, feminists working within these organisations in transforming them into gender-equitable institutions. The different feminist strategies of engagement or disengagement, and co-operation or confrontation are examined, vis-à-vis development institutions. Case studies from New Zealand, Australia, Canada, Vietnam, Uganda, Chile, and Morocco are presented. The importance of the relationship between 'insiders' (i.e. feminists working within development organisations) and 'outsiders' (i.e. organised women's movements) in attaining gender equitability within these organisations is a central theme of many of the articles.

Gender Training: The Source Book (1998) Sarah Cummings, Henk van Dam, and Minke Valk (eds.)
Royal Tropical Institute, KIT Press, PO Box 95001, 1090 HA Amsterdam, The Netherlands. Tel: +31 (20) 5688272; fax: +31 (20) 5688286, and Oxfam GB.
kitpress@kit.nl
www.kit.nl

With an emphasis on gender training as a transformative project, this book presents the experiences of Southern practitioners from South Asia, the Middle East, Eastern and Southern Africa, and South Africa involved in gender education and training. Gender training is presented as a tool to develop an understanding of gender power relations within organisations, and as a means to devise strategies for action and change within organisations. The authors emphasise the importance of a total organisational strategy for equitable change within which gender training can serve as one important component. The book also contains a bibliography of resources relevant to gender training (including workshop publications, manuals and methodologies, and case studies).

Policy, Politics and Gender: Women Gaining Ground (1998) Kathleen Staudt
Kumarian Press, 1294 Blue Hills Avenue, Bloomfield, CT. 06002 USA. Tel: +1 (860) 243 2098; orders tel: +1 (800) 289 2664; fax: +1 (860) 243 2867.
sales@kpbooks.com
www.kumarianpress.com

In this book, Staudt analyses development institutions and their policies in relation to their impact on women and stresses the importance of 'bringing politics back in'. In part one, the author provides an overview of the history of development thinking and women in development, and offers a framework to conceptualise different kinds of feminisms. In addition she examines the obstacles and strategies faced by gender advocates in national and international bureaucratic development institutions. In part two, mainstream policies related to education, work, reproductive health, and violence against women are examined through a gender lens. In the final section of the book, Staudt makes links between development institutions, the political contexts they are located within, and their gender mainstreaming policies.

Gender in Development Organisations (1997) Caroline Sweetman (ed.)
Oxfam GB, Oxfam House, John Smith Drive, Cowley, Oxford, OX4 2JY, UK
www.oxfam.org.uk/publications

This book examines some of the challenges, pitfalls, and rewards for development organisations that adopt, or are founded with, a 'gender agenda'. The experiences of national and international NGOs in Bangladesh, Lebanon, Lesotho, Zimbabwe, South Africa, and Uganda reveal the crucial significance of the organisation's own policies, procedures, structures, and culture, and of the wider cultural context within which the organisation operates, in determining the degree of success in its gender equity goals.

Getting Institutions Right for Women in Development (1997) Anne Marie Goetz (ed.) Zed Books, 7 Cynthia Street, London N1 9JF, UK.
www.zedbooks.co.uk

This book looks at the relationship between gendered aspects of development organisations (ranging from NGOs to state bureaucracies) and the gendered outcomes in the development process that continue to constrain or disadvantage women. The articles in the book look at the opportunities for development organisations to challenge institutional gender inequity. Some of the articles challenge the assumption that NGOs are inherently more gender-sensitive organisations, while others highlight the importance of individual agents in promoting gender equity within resistant organisations. There are also examples of women's organisations and the problems they face in challenging the norms of the wider cultural context within which they are located.

Institutions, Relations and Outcomes: Framework and Tools for Gender-Aware Planning (1996) Naila Kabeer and Ramya Subrahmanian, IDS Discussion Paper 357, Institute of Development Studies, University of Sussex, Brighton BN1 9RE, UK. Tel: +44 (0) 1273 678269; fax: +44 (0) 1273 621202
g.edwards@ids.ac.uk
www.ids.ac.uk/ids/bookshop/index.html

This paper details a framework that enables both a gender-aware analysis of institutions as well as the formulation of gender-aware policy. The authors use clear case studies to highlight the differences between gender-blind and gender-aware approaches to policy design and implementation. They discuss the difference between attempts to 'add-on' women in development policies and genuine mainstreaming that is inherently a transformatory project. The paper provides a step-by-step approach on how to examine the rules, activities, resources, people, and power located within institutions in order to achieve gender-sensitive policy planning, implementation, monitoring, and evaluation.

From WID to GAD: Conceptual Shifts in the Women and Development Discourse (1995) Shahrashoub Razavi and Carol Miller, UNRISD Occasional Paper.
Available online from: www.unrisd.org

This paper provides an introduction to WID by tracing the main trends in the way women's issues have been conceptualised in the development context. Part I of the paper explains the emergence of WID in the early 1970s. Part II looks at the analytical and intellectual underpinnings of the shift from WID to GAD.

Gender Mainstreaming: A Study of Efforts by the UNDP, the World Bank and the ILO to Institutionalise Gender Issues (1995) Shahrashoub Razavi and Carol Miller, UNRISD Occasional Paper.
Available online from: www.unrisd.org

This paper assesses the attempts of the three institutions to mainstream gender, and evaluates their achievements in the light of a) the external pressures and influences they are subject to; b) the organisational mandate and ideology; and c) the actual organisational procedures in place for mainstreaming gender. While some progress is noted, several problems and issues are raised, including inadequate resource allocation and ownership, and marginalisation of gender issues by the organisations.

The Elusive Agenda: Mainstreaming Women in Development (1995) Rounaq Jahan, Zed Books, 7 Cynthia Street, London N1 9JF, UK.
www.zedbooks.co.uk

This book is now well known for its description of gender mainstreaming as an 'agenda-setting' exercise, rather than an integrationist approach. Based on her study of the gender mainstreaming efforts of four international donor agencies, Jahan asks why progress towards transforming gender relations has been so slow. Her conclusions include the resistance by organisations to redistribute power and privileges that threaten entrenched male advantage, and their reluctance to commit to the goals of gender equality and women's empowerment.

'From Feminist Knowledge to Data for Development: The Bureaucratic Management of Information on Women and Development' (1994) Anne-Marie Goetz, *IDS Bulletin*, 25(2): 27-35.

The author discusses how feminist knowledge generated about women's roles, needs, and interests is de-politicised by the bureaucratic processes and rigid categories used within the development organisations that consume this knowledge. The result is that this knowledge may help in bringing women into development, but their diverse political needs are disregarded and do not feed into development organisations' policies and programmes. Goetz points to the nature of the categories used by development organisations as the root of the problem.

Reversed Realities (1994) Naila Kabeer, Verso.
www.versobooks.com

Kabeer traces the emergence of 'women' as a category in development, revealing the inherent, unexamined biases in mainstream development, with its emphasis on market-based economic growth, that further disadvantage poor women. The author argues for a bottom–up development perspective that starts with the interests of poor women. She analyses, among other things, the construction of power relations within the household, and strategies for the empowerment of women that emphasise both the importance of collective action by women and the central role that grass-roots NGOs can play in facilitating empowerment.

Gender Planning and Development: Theory, Practice and Training (1993) Caroline Moser Routledge, Taylor and Francis, 2 Park Square, Milton Park, Abingdon, Oxford, OX14 4RN, UK. Tel: +44 (0) 20 7017 6000; fax: +44 (0) 20 7017 6699.
www.routledge.com

This book argues for the importance of gender planning in development, the goal of which is the empowerment of women. Part one provides the rationale for gender planning and includes a discussion of the distinction between practical and strategic gender needs. It also includes Moser's widely recognised framework summarising policy approaches to women in development (i.e. welfare, equity, anti-poverty, efficiency, and empowerment). Part two outlines the methodological tools, procedures, and components that make up gender planning, such as gender training.

'The making of a field' (1990) Irene Tinker, in *Persistent Inequalities: Women and World Development*, Irene Tinker (ed.),
Oxford University Press, Oxford University Press Bookshop, 116 High Street, Oxford, OX1 4BZ. Tel: +44 (0) 1865 242913; fax: +44 (0) 1865 241701.
bookshop.uk@oup.com
www.oup.com

Writing at the start of the 1990s, Tinker, a pioneer in the field of women in development, provides an overview of how 'women in development' came into force. The author discusses the role and challenges faced by the three major players in the field: advocates, practitioners, and scholars. She looks at new developments beyond the dominant frameworks of time-welfare and efficiency, such as the importance of women's empowerment (through organising), a critique of women's demands for equality with men on the grounds of sameness, and the gendered analysis of political institutions.

Development, Crises and Alternative Visions: Third World Women's Perspectives (1987) Gita Sen and Caren Grown,
Earthscan, 8-12 Camden High Street, London, NW1 0JH, UK. Tel: +44 (0)20 7387 8558; fax: +44 (0)20 7387 8998.
earthinfo@earthscan.co.uk
www.earthscan.co.uk

This book is by two members of DAWN (Development Alternatives with Women for a New Era), a network of largely Southern activists and researchers. It is one of the earliest works denouncing the adverse impact of the gender-blindness of development policies on the lives of women in the economic South. The economic growth policies espoused by agencies like the World Bank, in the name of development, come under severe criticism, and the authors emphasise the importance of women's roles and voices in overcoming the devastating effects of these policies. The book also looks at the strategies and methods for women to move towards gender equality.

Websites

Siyanda
www.siyanda.org

Siyanda is an online database of gender and development materials, with new material on gender equality and mainstreaming being regularly added. It also enables gender practitioners to share ideas, experiences, and resources with each other.

BRIDGE
www.bridge.ids.ac.uk

BRIDGE supports gender advocacy and mainstreaming efforts by bridging the gaps between theory, policy, and practice with accessible and diverse gender information in print and online. The site has been set up as a 'virtual bookcase' where copies of all BRIDGE publications can be downloaded. Themes include Country Profiles, Economics, Governance, and Poverty.

Women Watch
www.un.org/womenwatch

WomenWatch is a central gateway to information and resources on the promotion of gender equality and the empowerment of women throughout the United Nations system, including the United Nations Secretariat, regional commissions, funds, programmes, specialised agencies, and academic and research institutions. It is a joint United Nations project created in March 1997 to provide Internet space for global gender equality issues and to support implementation of the 1995 Beijing Platform for Action. The website now also provides information on the outcomes of, as well as efforts to incorporate gender perspectives into follow-up to global conferences.

The Men's Bibliography
http://mensbiblio.xyonline.net

The Men's Bibliography is a comprehensive and up-to-date bibliography of writing on men, masculinities, gender, and sexualities. The Men's Bibliography lists over 15,000 books and articles, sorted into over 30 major subject areas.

Oxfam GB's website pages on its gender work
www.oxfam.org.uk/what_we_do/issues/gender/index.htm
Oxfam GB's website pages on gender equality and men
www.oxfam.org.uk/what_we_do/issues/gender/gem/index.htm

These pages include information on why Oxfam works with men on gender equality, workshop material on working with men, and links to other websites and resources on gender equality and men.

ActionAid UK's website pages on its gender work
www.actionaid.org.uk/index.asp?page_id=417

Electronic resources

Gender and Diversity Resources Kit (2005) Gender and Development (GAD) Network, London, UK.
For more information on the CD-ROM email: gadnetwork@womankind.org.uk

This CD-ROM is the outcome of a two-phase GAD Network research project carried out between January 2004 and March 2005. The project was aimed at learning more about the emphasis on 'diversity' across UK development organisations and its possible implications for gender mainstreaming. The CD-ROM contains an overview of the project and its main findings; a 'think piece' on gender and diversity; case studies that explore in greater detail the practical approaches and methodologies being developed for working on diversity issues in rights-based programming; an overview summarising some of the approaches being used to address issues of diversity. There is also a resources section for further information on the issues covered.

Gender Myths (2004) BRIDGE.
www.bridge.ids.ac.uk/docs/in%20brief_myths.pdf

Drawing together highlights from a conference held at the Institute of Development Studies, UK in 2003, the discussions in 'Gender Myths' focus on how to move beyond the gender stereotypes that feminists have created to counter pre-existing gender stereotypes in development. These stereotypes have taken on the quality of myths and are treated as sacrosanct. The discussion centres on how to promote gender equality better by moving beyond these simplistic stereotypes.

Gender Mainstreaming: Can it Work for Women's Rights? (2004) AWID.
www.awid.org/publications/OccasionalPapers/spotlight3_en.pdf

Four AWID members engaged with gender mainstreaming draw on their experiences to discuss what has gone wrong with gender mainstreaming, and why it has failed to make any progress in delivering equality to women. Common strands of arguments include the fact that gender mainstreaming has been reduced from a transformative project to a technical fix, and that confusion over what it actually means has rendered women's rights and gender equality invisible.

'Approaches to institutionalising gender' (1997) *Development and Gender In Brief*, Issue 5, BRIDGE.
www.bridge.ids.ac.uk/Dgb5.html

This issue reviews approaches to institutionalising gender issues in both government and non-government organisations and looks at what happens to feminist concepts, such as empowerment, when they enter the mainstream.

Oxfam's Policy on Gender Equality (2003).
www.oxfam.org.uk/what_we_do/issues/gender/downloads/gender_policy2003.pdf

This provides the rationale for Oxfam's organisational commitment to gender equality.

ActionAid's Gender Policy (2000).
www.actionaid.org.uk/wps/content/documents/genderpolicy.doc

This details ActionAid's organisation-wide strategies to mainstream gender equality and women's empowerment.

Gender is Everyone's Business: Programming with Men to Achieve Gender Equality (2002) James Lang.
www.oxfam.org.uk/what_we_do/issues/gender/gem/downloads/GEMwkshprep.pdf

This is a workshop report from Oxfam GB's 'Gender Equality and Men' (GEM) project that details the workshop process and participants, conceptual framework, good practices and lessons learned from working with men and boys, and recommendations for next steps.

Reflections on Experiences of Evaluating Gender Equality (2003) Ted Freeman, Britha Mikkelsen *et al.*
www.sida.se/content/1/c6/01/88/28/44717%20UTV%20Studies%202003-01.pdf

This report reflects on Sida's (Swedish International Development Co-operation Agency) evaluation of its gender equality work in Nicaragua, South Africa, and Bangladesh, with the aim of contributing to current debates on gender mainstreaming. The report discusses the challenges of evaluating concepts like gender equality, gender mainstreaming, and empowerment when donor agencies and partner countries debate their very meaning. It discusses the implications of conducting such evaluations when the definitions of what is being measured are provided by the evaluation team rather than primary stakeholders. The report also identifies challenges in gender mainstreaming such as 'who owns gender mainstreaming if it is not working' and the gap between stated policy and practices.

The Role of National Mechanisms in Promoting Gender Equality and the Empowerment of Women: Report of the Expert Group Meeting (2004) United Nations Division for the Advancement of Women.
www.un.org/womenwatch/daw/egm/nationalm2004/docs/EGM%20final%20report.26-jan-05.pdf

This report emerged out of an Expert Group Meeting arranged by the UN Division for the Advancement of Women (DAW) to contribute to the review and appraisal of the implementation of the Beijing Platform for Action (BPfA). The focus was on the BPfA commitment to strengthen national mechanisms for the advancement of women. The meeting considered the changing contexts as well as the achievements of different types of institutional mechanisms for the advancement of women, in formulation, implementation, and monitoring of national strategies for gender equality and empowerment of women, and in facilitating gender mainstreaming in all national policy areas. It further identified good practices and continuing challenges faced by national mechanisms.

Gender Equality and Mainstreaming in the Policy and Practice of the UK Department for International Development (2003) A briefing from the UK Gender and Development (GAD) Network.
www.siyanda.org/docs/gadn_dfidgenderpolicy.pdf

This report analyses DFID's progress in gender mainstreaming and the implementation of its commitments under the Convention for Elimination of All Forms of Discrimination Against Women (CEDAW), the Beijing Platform for Action and the Millennium Development Goals (MDGs). It is based on a review of DFID documents, interviews with DFID staff, and surveys of GAD Network members' experiences with DFID. The findings were that DFID's rights-based approach is one of its greatest strengths. However, policy commitments to gender equality have been implemented unevenly. The way gender inequality is addressed is inconsistent, vacillating between a rights-based approach and one based on efficiency. Recommendations include: producing clearer information on gender equality spending; strengthening DFID institutional capacity for gender mainstreaming, with new structures, monitoring, training, and better dissemination and knowledge management of high quality work on gender.

United Nations Development Programme Gender Mainstreaming tools
www.undp.org/gender/tools.htm

This website provides an array of documents created and utilised by UNDP and other UN agencies in their efforts to mainstream gender. Available documents on the site include gender briefing and training tools, a guide on how to develop a gender mainstreaming strategy, a gender mainstreaming manual, as well as information on where gender training courses are available.

The Commonwealth Secretariat Gender Management Systems Series
www.thecommonwealth.org/gender (click on 'Publications' in the left hand column then 'Gender Management Systems series')

This website provides free access to a series of practical, training-oriented resources by the Commonwealth Secretariat on gender mainstreaming. These include: an Action Guide and Trainer's Guide on gender mainstreaming approaches and gender training; the Gender Management System Toolkit; Handbook; Using Gender-Sensitive Indicators; and guides on how to mainstream gender in education, development planning, finance, trade and industry, public services, etc.

The Commonwealth Secretariat Gender Mainstreaming Series on Development Issues
www.thecommonwealth.org/gender (click on 'Publications' in the left hand column, then on 'Gender mainstreaming series on development issues')

This links to a number of books, pamphlets, and papers published by the Commonwealth Secretariat on gender mainstreaming aimed at governments, policy makers, development professionals, and others. Titles include gender mainstreaming in poverty eradication, the health sector, HIV/AIDS, and budgets, and an integrated approach to combating gender-based violence.

Gender Manual: A Practical Guide for Development Policy Makers and Practitioners (2002) Helen Derbyshire.
www.dfid.gov.uk/pubs/files/gender manual.pdf

Designed for use by development practitioners who are not specialists in gender, the aim of this manual is to help in organisational efforts to mainstream gender. The manual is divided into three main sections. Section one deals with the background ideas and concepts of gender mainstreaming and explains the importance of mainstreaming gender. Section two provides a summary of the key steps in gender mainstreaming. Section three contains practical tools and guidelines on how to mainstream gender (such as the use of gender-disaggregated data and gender-sensitive analysis, organisational capacity building, and change).

Organisations

Gender at Work
www.genderatwork.org

The Gender at Work initiative is a knowledge and capacity building network focused on gender and institutional change. The network works with development and human rights practitioners, researchers, and policy makers. It aims to develop new theory and practice on how organisations can change gender-biased institutional rules (the distribution of power, privileges, and rights), values (norms and attitudes), and practices. In addition to information on the network and a discussion forum, the network's website offers access to the network's current analyses and resources.

The Association for Women's Rights in Development (AWID)
Toronto Secretariat: 215 Spadina Ave., Suite 150, Toronto, Ontario, M5T 2C7, Canada. Tel: +1 416 594 3773; fax: +1 416 594 0330.
awid@awid.org
www.awid.org

AWID is an international membership organisation connecting, informing, and mobilising people and organisations committed to achieving gender equality, sustainable development, and women's human rights. Their goal is to cause policy, institutional, and individual change that will improve the lives of women and girls everywhere. They aim to do this by facilitating ongoing debates on fundamental and provocative issues as well as by building the individual and organisational capacities of those working for women's empowerment and social justice.

Womankind Worldwide
32-37, 2nd Floor, Development House, 56-64 Leonard Street, London EC2A 4JX, UK. Tel: +44 (0)20 7549 0360; fax: +44 (0) 20 7549 0361.
info@womankind.org.uk
www.womankind.org.uk

Womankind Worldwide is a UK-based charity dedicated to women's development and women's human rights globally. Womankind has developed programmes in partnership with local community groups, to tackle women's inequality in many of the world's poorest places. These programmes are called the Four Literacies — Word Literacy, Money Literacy, Body Literacy, and Civil Literacy — and they work to unlock women's potential and maximise their ability to make decisions in their own lives, the lives of their family, as well as in the future of their community and country. Womankind works with 70 partner organisations in 20 countries, spanning Africa, South Asia, Central and South America, and Europe.

Women In Development Europe (WIDE)
rue de la Science 10, 1000 Brussels, Belgium. Tel: +32 2 5459070; fax: +32 2 5127342.
info@wide-network.org
www.eurosur.org/wide/home.htm

WIDE is a European network of development NGOs, gender specialists, and human rights activists. It monitors and influences international economic and development policy and practice from a feminist perspective. WIDE's work is grounded on women's rights as the basis for the development of a more just and democratic world order. WIDE strives for a world based on gender equality and social justice that ensures equal rights for all, as well as equal access to resources and opportunities in all spheres of political, social, and economic life.